New Perspectives on

Microsoft® Office Outlook® 2003

Essentials

THOMSON
™
COURSE TECHNOLOGY

Australia • Canada • Mexico • Singapore • Spain • United Kingdom • United States

What does this logo mean?

It means this courseware has been approved by the Microsoft® Office Specialist Program to be among the finest available for learning Microsoft Outlook®. It also means that upon completion of this courseware, you may be prepared to take an exam for Microsoft Office Specialist qualification.

What is a Microsoft Office Specialist?

A Microsoft Office Specialist is an individual who has passed exams for certifying his or her skills in one or more of the Microsoft Office desktop applications such as Microsoft Word, Microsoft Excel, Microsoft PowerPoint, Microsoft Outlook®, Microsoft Access, or Microsoft Project. The Microsoft Office Specialist Program is the only program in the world approved by Microsoft for testing proficiency in Microsoft Office desktop applications and Microsoft Project.* This testing program can be a valuable asset in any job search or career advancement.

More Information:

To learn more about becoming a Microsoft Office Specialist, visit www.microsoft.com/officespecialist

To learn about other Microsoft Office Specialist approved courseware from Course Technology, visit www.course.com/newperspectives/teacherslounge

www.course.com/NewPerspectives

New Perspectives on

Microsoft® Office Outlook® 2003

Essentials

Robin M. Romer

THOMSON

COURSE TECHNOLOGY

Australia • Canada • Mexico • Singapore • Spain • United Kingdom • United States

THOMSON

COURSE TECHNOLOGY

New Perspectives on Microsoft® Office Outlook 2003—Essentials
is published by Course Technology.

Managing Editor: Rachel Goldberg	**Associate Product Manager:** Emilie Perreault	**Production Editor:** Jennifer Goguen
Senior Product Manager: Kathy Finnegan	**Editorial Assistant:** Shana Rosenthal	**Composition:** GEX Publishing Services
Senior Product Manager: Amanda Young Shelton	**Marketing Manager:** Joy Stark	**Text Designer:** Steve Deschene
Product Manager: Karen Stevens	**Developmental Editor:** Katherine T. Pinard	**Cover Designer:** Nancy Goulet
Product Manager: Brianna Germain		

Preface

Real, Thought-Provoking, Engaging, Dynamic, Interactive—these are just a few of the words that are used to describe the New Perspectives Series' approach to learning and building computer skills.

Without our critical-thinking and problem-solving methodology, computer skills could be learned but not retained. By teaching with a case-based approach, the New Perspectives Series challenges students to apply what they've learned to real-life situations.

Our ever-growing community of users understands why they're learning what they're learning. Now you can too!

See what instructors and students are saying about the best-selling New Perspectives Series:

"The New Perspectives format is a pleasure to use. The Quick Checks and the tutorial Review Assignments help students view topics from a real world perspective."
— Craig Shaw, Central Community College – Hastings

"I have used books from the New Perspectives series for about ten years now. I haven't been able to find anything else that approaches their quality when it comes to covering intermediate and advanced software application topics."
— Karleen Nordquist, College of St. Benedict & St. John's University

www.course.com/NewPerspectives

Why *New Perspectives* will work for you

Context
Each tutorial begins with a problem presented in a "real-world" case that is meaningful to students. The case sets the scene to help students understand what they will do in the tutorial.

Hands-on Approach
Each tutorial is divided into manageable sessions that combine reading and hands-on, step-by-step work. Screenshots—now 20% larger for enhanced readability—help guide students through the steps. **Trouble?** tips anticipate common mistakes or problems to help students stay on track and continue with the tutorial.

Review

Review
In New Perspectives, retention is a key component to learning. At the end of each session, a series of Quick Check questions helps students test their understanding of the concepts before moving on. And now each tutorial contains an end-of-tutorial summary and a list of key terms for further reinforcement.

Apply

Assessment
Engaging and challenging Review Assignments and Case Problems have always been a hallmark feature of the New Perspectives Series. Now we've added new features to make them more accessible! Colorful icons and brief descriptions accompany the exercises, making it easy to understand, at a glance, both the goal and level of challenge a particular assignment holds.

Reference Window

Task Reference

Reference
While contextual learning is excellent for retention, there are times when students will want a high-level understanding of how to accomplish a task. Within each tutorial, Reference Windows appear before a set of steps to provide a succinct summary and preview of how to perform a task. In addition, a complete Task Reference at the back of the book provides quick access to information on how to carry out common tasks. Finally, each book includes a combination Glossary/Index to promote easy reference of material.

Reinforce

Lab Assignments
Certain tutorials in this book contain Lab Assignments, which provide additional reinforcement of important skills in a simulated environment. These labs have been hailed by students and teachers alike for years as the most comprehensive and accurate on the market. Great for pre-work or remediation, the labs help students learn concepts and skills in a structured environment.

Student Online Companion
This book has an accompanying online companion Web site designed to enhance learning. This Web site includes:
- Student Data Files
- PowerPoint presentations

Certification
This logo on the front of this book means that this book has been independently reviewed and approved by ProCert Labs. If you are interested in acquiring Microsoft Office Specialist certification, you may use this book as courseware in your preparation. For more information on this certification, go to www.microsoft.com/officespecialist.

www.course.com/NewPerspectives

New Perspectives offers an entire system of instruction

The New Perspectives Series is more than just a handful of books. It's a complete system of offerings:

New Perspectives catalog
Our online catalog is never out of date! Go to the catalog link on our Web site to check out our available titles, request a desk copy, download a book preview, or locate online files.

Coverage to meet your needs!
Whether you're looking for just a small amount of coverage or enough to fill a semester-long class, we can provide you with a textbook that meets your needs.

- Brief books typically cover the essential skills in just 2 to 4 tutorials.
- Introductory books build and expand on those skills and contain an average of 5 to 8 tutorials.
- Comprehensive books are great for a full-semester class, and contain 9 to 12+ tutorials.
- Power Users or Advanced books are perfect for a highly accelerated introductory class or a second course in a given topic.

So if the book you're holding does not provide the right amount of coverage for you, there's probably another offering available. Go to our Web site or contact your Course Technology sales representative to find out what else we offer.

Instructor Resources

We offer more than just a book. We have all the tools you need to enhance your lectures, check students' work, and generate exams in a new, easier-to-use and completely revised package. This book's Instructor's Manual, ExamView testbank, PowerPoint presentations, data files, solution files, figure files, and a sample syllabus are all available on a single CD-ROM or for downloading at www.course.com.

How will your students master Microsoft Office?
SAM (Skills Assessment Manager) 2003 helps you energize your class exams and training assignments by allowing students to learn and test important computer skills in an active, hands-on environment. With SAM 2003, you create powerful interactive exams on critical Microsoft Office 2003 applications, including Word, Excel, Access, and PowerPoint. The exams simulate the application environment, allowing your students to demonstrate their knowledge and to think through the skills by performing real-world tasks. Designed to be used with the New Perspectives Series, SAM 2003 includes built-in page references so students can create study guides that match the New Perspectives textbooks you use in class. Powerful administrative options allow you to schedule exams and assignments, secure your tests, and run reports with almost limitless flexibility. Find out more about SAM 2003 by going to www.course.com or speaking with your Course Technology sales representative.

Distance Learning

Enhance your course with any of our online learning platforms. Go to www.course.com or speak with your Course Technology sales representative to find the platform or the content that's right for you.

www.course.com/NewPerspectives

New Perspectives on

Microsoft® Office Outlook® 2003

Read This Before You Begin: Tutorials 1–3

To the Student

Data Files

To complete Outlook Tutorials 1 and 2, you need the starting student Data Files. Your instructor will either provide you with these Data Files or ask you to obtain them yourself.

Outlook Tutorials 1 and 2 require the folders shown in the next column to complete the Tutorials, Review Assignments, and Case Problems. You will need to copy these folders from a file server, a standalone computer, or the Web to the drive and folder where you will be storing your Data Files. Your instructor will tell you which computer, drive letter, and folder(s) contain the files you need. You can also download the files by going to www.course.com; see the inside back or front cover for more information on downloading the files, or ask your instructor or technical support person for assistance.

If you are storing your Data Files on floppy disks, you will need **four** blank, formatted, high-density disks for this tutorial. Label your disks as shown, and place on them the folder(s) indicated.

▼ **Outlook 2003: Data Disk 1**
Tutorial.01\Tutorial folder

▼ **Outlook 2003: Data Disk 2**
Tutorial.01\Review folder
Tutorial.01\Cases folder

▼ **Outlook 2003: Data Disk 3**
Tutorial.02\Tutorial folder
Tutorial.02\Review folder

▼ **Outlook 2003: Data Disk 4**
Tutorial.02\Cases folder

When you begin a tutorial, refer to the Student Data Files section at the bottom of the tutorial opener page, which indicates which folders and files you need for the tutorial. Each end-of-tutorial exercise also indicates the files you need to complete that exercise.

To the Instructor

The Data Files are available on the Instructor Resources CD for this title. Follow the instructions in the Help file on the CD to install the programs to your network or standalone computer. See the "To the Student" section above for information on how to set up the Data Files that accompany this text.

You are granted a license to copy the Data Files to any computer or computer network used by students who have purchased this book.

System Requirements

If you are going to work through this book using your own computer, you need:

• **Computer System** Microsoft Windows 2000, Windows XP or higher must be installed on your computer. These tutorials assume a typical installation of Microsoft Office 2003. Also, you need Windows Messenger installed on your computer. Windows

Messenger comes with Windows XP and is available to download from the Microsoft Web site if you are using Windows 2000.

• **Data Disk** You will not be able to complete the tutorials or exercises in this book using your own computer until you have the necessary starting Data Files.

www.course.com/NewPerspectives

Objectives

Session 1.1
- Start and exit Outlook
- Explore the Outlook window
- Navigate between Outlook components
- Create and edit contact information
- Create and send e-mail messages

Session 1.2
- Read and respond to e-mail messages
- Attach files to e-mail messages
- File, sort, save, and archive messages

Communicating with Outlook 2003

Sending and Receiving E-mail Messages

Case

The Express Lane

The Express Lane is a complete and affordable online grocery store in the San Francisco Bay Area, specializing in natural and organic foods. Alan Gregory and Lora Shaw began The Express Lane in 1998 in response to what they saw as a growing need for more online grocery shopping services. Customers span all income and educational levels, ages, and locations.

Unlike traditional groceries, The Express Lane does not have a storefront where customers come to shop. Instead it stores both packaged goods and fresh produce in its warehouse. Customers place orders using e-mail or the company's Web site, or fax. The Express Lane staff then selects and packs the requested items, bills the customer's credit card for the cost of the groceries plus a $5 service fee, and delivers the groceries to the customer's front door within 12 to 24 hours. To coordinate these activities, The Express Lane relies on **Microsoft Outlook**, an information management and communication program.

To help manage their company's growth, Alan and Lora hire you to assist them with the variety of tasks they perform using Outlook. In this tutorial, you'll explore the Outlook window and its components. You'll use e-mail to send information about increasing an order to a supplier. You'll also set up contact information for suppliers and The Express Lane staff. Then you'll receive, read, and respond to e-mail messages. Finally you'll organize messages by filing, filtering, sorting, and archiving them.

Student Data Files

▼Tutorial.01

▽ **Tutorial folder**

Sales.xls

▽ **Review folder**

Tea.doc

▽ **Cases folder**

Amendments.doc

Exploring Outlook

Microsoft Outlook is a powerful information manager. You can use Outlook to perform a wide range of communication and organizational tasks, such as sending, receiving, and filing e-mail; organizing contact information; scheduling appointments, events, and meetings; creating a to-do list and delegating tasks; and writing notes.

There are six main components in Outlook. The **Mail** component is a message/communication tool for receiving, sending, storing, and managing e-mail. The three mail folders you will use the most often are the Inbox folder, which stores messages you have received; the Outbox folder, which stores messages you have written but not sent; and the Sent Items folder, which stores copies of messages you have sent. You also can create other folders to save and organize e-mail you've received and written. The **Calendar** component is a scheduling tool for planning appointments, events, and meetings. The **Contacts** component is an address book for compiling postal addresses, phone numbers, e-mail and Web addresses, and other personal and business information about people and businesses with whom you communicate. The **Notes** component is a notepad for jotting down ideas and thoughts that you can group, sort, and categorize. The **Tasks** component is a to-do list for organizing and tracking items you need to complete or delegate. The **Journal** component is a diary for recording your activities, such as time spent talking on the phone, sending an e-mail message, or working on a document. As you work with these components, you create items such as e-mail messages, appointments, contacts, tasks, journal entries, and notes. An **item** is the basic element that holds information in Outlook, similar to a file in other programs. Items are organized into **folders**. Unlike folders in Windows Explorer, Outlook folders are available only from within Outlook.

Starting Outlook

You start Outlook the same way as any other program—using the Start menu. If Outlook is the default e-mail program on your computer, you can also click the E-mail link in the pinned items list at the top of the Start menu to start the program.

To start Outlook:

1. Click the **Start** button on the taskbar, point to **All Programs**, point to **Microsoft Office**, and then click **Microsoft Office Outlook 2003**. After a short pause, the Outlook program window appears. The pane on the right displays **Outlook Today**, a view of Outlook that shows your appointments, tasks, and number of e-mail messages you have.

   Trouble? If you don't see the Microsoft Office Outlook 2003 option on the Microsoft Office submenu, look for it on a different submenu or as an option on the All Programs menu, or click the E-mail Microsoft Office Outlook option at the top of the Start menu. If you still can't find the Microsoft Office Outlook 2003 option, ask your instructor or technical support person for help.

   Trouble? If a dialog box opens, indicating that you need to set up an e-mail account, click the Cancel button and continue with Step 2.

   Trouble? If a dialog box opens, asking whether you want to import e-mail messages and addresses from Outlook Express or another e-mail program, click the No button.

   Trouble? If a dialog box opens, asking whether you want to make Outlook the default manager for Mail, News, and Contacts, click the No button.

   Trouble? If a dialog box opens, asking whether you want to AutoArchive your old items now, click the No button.

2. If necessary, click the **Maximize** button 🔲. Figure 1-1 shows the maximized Outlook window.

Outlook Today   Figure 1-1

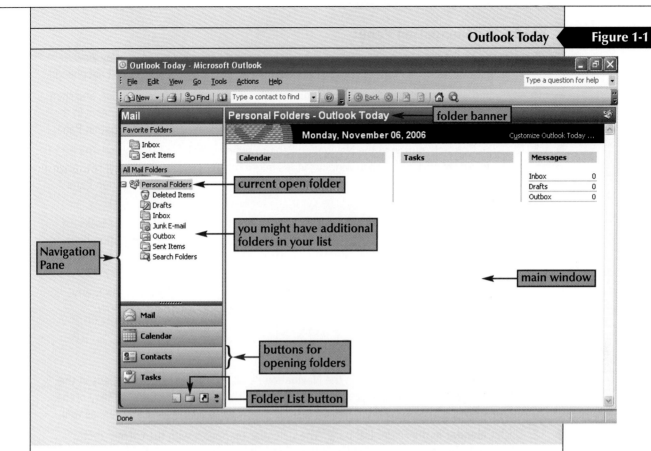

The Outlook window contains some elements that might be familiar to you from other programs, such as Word or Excel. Other elements are specific to Outlook, including:

- **Navigation Pane.** A central tool for accessing Outlook folders or files and folders on your computer or network that contains buttons to access additional panes within the Navigation Pane.
- **Folder List.** A hierarchy of the Outlook folders that you use to store and organize items; also provides a way to navigate among the Outlook folders. The Folder List is not shown in Figure 1-1; you'll work with it later in this tutorial.
- **Folder banner.** A bar at the top of the main window that displays the name of the open folder.
- **Main window.** The display of items stored in the selected folder; may be divided into panes. For example, the center pane of the Inbox main window displays a list of e-mail messages in the Inbox, and the right pane displays the contents of the selected e-mail message.

No matter which component you use, these elements of the Outlook window work in the same way. You can use the View menu to display or hide any of these elements, depending on your needs and preferences.

Navigating Between Outlook Components

You can click any button in the Navigation Pane to display that folder's contents in the main window. The Navigation Pane contains buttons for the most commonly used Outlook folders—Mail, Calendar, Contacts, Tasks, Notes, Folder List, and Shortcuts. Depending on the size of your monitor, the Notes, Folder List, and Shortcuts buttons may appear as icons at the bottom of the Navigation Pane rather than as bars with the name of the pane displayed. You click a button to display its contents in the Navigation Pane.

To use the Navigation Pane:

► **1.** Click the **Mail** button in the Navigation Pane. The Personal Folders - Outlook Today view appears in the main window. If the Mail button was already selected, your view will not change.

► **2.** Click the **Calendar** button in the Navigation Pane to switch to the Calendar folder, and then click the **Day** button on the Standard toolbar, if necessary. The daily planner appears in the main window, and the current month's calendar appears at the top of the Navigation Pane.

► **3.** Click the **Contacts** button in the Navigation Pane to switch to the Contacts folder. The list of contacts is displayed in the main window; yours might be empty, but you will still see letter buttons along the right side that you use to scroll the contacts list. The Navigation Pane contains the Current View pane.

► **4.** Click the **Tasks** button in the Navigation Pane to switch to the Tasks folder. The tasks list appears in the main window and the Current View pane appears in the Navigation Pane.

A second way to navigate between folders is with the Folder List. You can click any folder name in the Folder List to display the folder's contents in the main window.

To navigate with the Folder List:

► **1.** Click the **Folder List** button 🗀 in the Navigation Pane. The Folder List pane opens at the top of the Navigation Pane, displaying icons for each of the folders in Outlook. Many of them are the same as the folders listed in the Mail pane, but there are additional folders as well.

► **2.** Click **Calendar** in the Folder List pane. The Calendar reappears with the current month's calendar in the top pane and the Folder List pane above the Navigation Pane buttons.

► **3.** Click **Inbox** in the Folder List pane. The Inbox folder opens in the main window. If there are any messages in your Inbox, the contents of the selected message might appear in the Reading pane to the right of or below the main window. See Figure 1-2.

Figure 1-2 ▶ **Inbox folder**

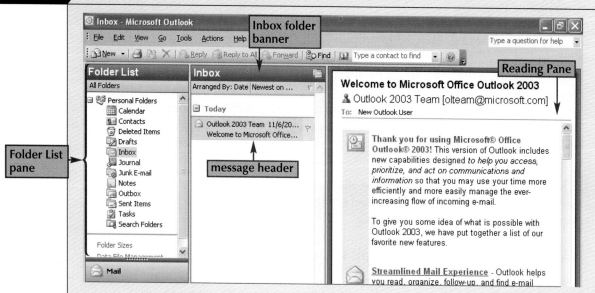

The main window currently displays the contents of the Inbox folder, where you receive, create, and send e-mail messages.

Creating and Sending E-mail Messages

E-mail, the electronic transfer of messages between computers, is a simple and inexpensive way to communicate with friends around the corner, family across the country, and colleagues in the same building or around the world. The messages you send are delivered immediately and stored until recipients can read those messages at their convenience. The Express Lane staff uses e-mail to correspond with its customers, suppliers, and each other because it is fast, convenient, and inexpensive. In addition, it saves the company the cost of paper, ink or toner, and other supplies.

Before you can send and receive e-mail messages with Outlook, you must have access to an e-mail server or Internet service provider (ISP), an e-mail address, and a password. An **e-mail address** is a user ID and a host name separated by the @ symbol. A **user ID** (or user name or account name) is a unique name that identifies you to your mail server. The **host name** consists of the name of your ISP's computer on the Internet plus its domain or level. For example, in the e-mail address "alan@theexpresslane.com," "alan" is the user ID and "theexpresslane.com" is the host name. Although many people might use the same host, each user ID is unique, enabling the host to distinguish one user from another. A **password** is a private code that you enter to access your account. (In this tutorial, you'll use your own e-mail address to send all messages.)

If you haven't already set up an Outlook mail account, you'll need to do so now by using the E-mail Accounts Wizard and completing the following steps.

To set up an Outlook mail account:

▶ 1. Click **Tools** on the menu bar, and then click **E-mail Accounts**. The first dialog box of the E-mail Accounts Wizard opens. Here, you choose whether you want to create a new account or modify an existing one.

▶ 2. Click the **Add a new e-mail account** option button, and then click the **Next** button. The Server Type dialog box of the E-mail Accounts Wizard opens and lists various server types.

▶ 3. Select the type of server you will use to access your e-mail, and then click the **Next** button. The Internet E-mail Settings dialog box varies, depending on the type of server you selected. Figure 1-3 shows the options when the POP3 server type is selected in the Server Type dialog box.

| Internet E-mail Settings dialog box for POP3 server type account | Figure 1-3 |

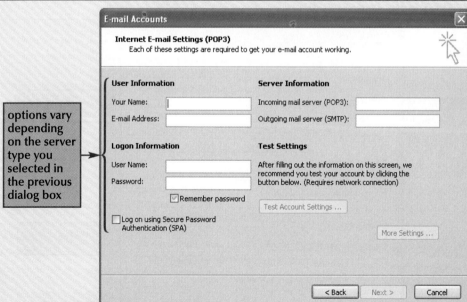

options vary depending on the server type you selected in the previous dialog box

▶ 4. Enter the requested information in the Internet E-mail Settings dialog box, and then click the **More Settings** button. The Internet E-mail Settings dialog box opens with the General tab on top.

5. Type your name in the Mail Account text box, press the **spacebar**, and then type **E-mail Account**. This is the name by which you will refer to this e-mail account in Outlook.

6. Click the **OK** button, and then click the **Test Account Settings** button. Outlook opens the Test Account Settings dialog box and verifies that your e-mail account works.

   Trouble? If you are unsure of what information to enter in the Internet E-mail Settings dialog box or if the test fails, ask your instructor or technical support person for help.

8. Click the **Close** button in the Test Account Settings dialog box, click the **Next** button in the Internet E-mail Settings dialog box, and then click the **Finish** button to set up your account based on the information you entered.

Choosing a Message Format

Outlook can send and receive messages in three formats: HTML, Rich Text, and Plain Text. Although you specify one of these formats as the default for your messages, you can always switch formats for an individual message. HTML provides the most formatting features and options (text formatting, numbering, bullets, alignment, horizontal lines, backgrounds, HTML styles, and Web pages). Rich Text provides some formatting options (text formatting, bullets, and alignment). With both HTML and Rich Text, some recipients will not be able to see the formatting if their e-mail software is not set up to handle formatted messages. Plain Text messages include no formatting, and the recipient specifies which font is used for the message. When you reply to a message, Outlook uses the same format in which the message was created, unless you specify otherwise. For example, if you reply to a message sent to you in Plain Text, Outlook sends the response in Plain Text.

You'll set the message format to HTML so you can customize your messages.

To choose a default message format:

1. Click **Tools** on the menu bar, and then click **Options**. The Options dialog box opens.

2. Click the **Mail Format** tab.

3. If necessary, click the **Compose in this message format** list arrow, and then click **HTML**.

4. If necessary, click the **Use Microsoft Office Word 2003 to edit e-mail messages** check box to insert a check mark. See Figure 1-4.

| Figure 1-4 | Mail Format tab in the Options dialog box |

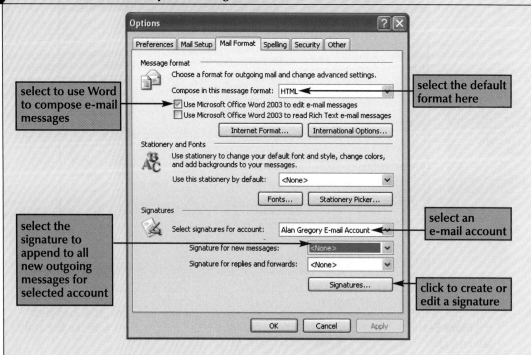

Now each time you create a message, Outlook will use the HTML format, unless you select a different format for that message. Because you selected HTML as your message format, you can customize your messages with a formatted signature. You'll do that before closing the Options dialog box.

Adding a Signature

A **signature** is text that is automatically added to every e-mail message you send. A signature can contain any text you want. For example, you might create a signature with your name, job title, company name, and phone number. The Express Lane might create a signature containing a paragraph that describes how to order groceries. You can also create more than one signature and then use the Signature button on the Standard toolbar to select which one you want to include in a particular message. If you have more than one e-mail account, you can create different signatures for each e-mail account you have set up. Although you can attach a signature to a message in any format, the HTML and Rich Text formats enable you to apply font and paragraph formatting. For now, you'll create a simple signature with your name and the company name. Note that the figures in this book will show the name Alan Gregory, whose e-mail address is alan@theexpresslane.com.

To create a signature:

1. Click the **Signatures** button on the Mail Format tab in the Options dialog box, and then click the **New** button in the Create Signature dialog box. The Create New Signature dialog box opens.

2. Type your name in the Enter a name for your new signature text box, click the **Start with a blank signature** option button if necessary, and then click the **Next** button. The Edit Signature dialog box opens with the insertion point blinking in the large text box.

3. Type your name, press the **Enter** key, and then type **The Express Lane**. See Figure 1-5.

Edit Signature dialog box ◄ **Figure 1-5**

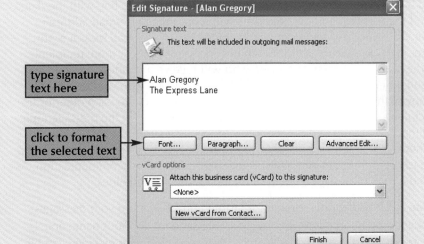

Next, you'll change the format of part of the signature.

4. Select **The Express Lane**, click the **Font** button, change the font to **10-point, Bold Italic, Arial**, and then click the **OK** button in the Font dialog box. The selected text is reformatted.

5. Click the **Finish** button. The Create Signature dialog box appears again, with your new signature listed and selected in the Signature box, and a preview of the selected signature.

6. Click the **OK** button to return to the Options dialog box.

   You'll add your signature to new messages you create, but not to messages you respond to.

7. Click the **Select signatures for account** list arrow, and then click your e-mail account name (your name, followed by "E-mail Account" if you set up your account in this tutorial).

8. If necessary, click the **Signature for new messages** list arrow, and then click your name.

9. If necessary, click the **Signature for replies and forwards** list arrow, and then click **<None>**.

10. Click the **Apply** button. If you had more than one e-mail account, you could click the Select signatures for account list arrow again, click the name of another e-mail account, and then repeat Steps 7 and 8 to create a signature for that account.

11. Click the **OK** button.

Using Stationery

Stationery templates are HTML files that include complementary fonts, background colors, and images for your outgoing e-mail messages. They also increase the size of your message. To use one of the stationery templates that comes with Outlook, including announcements, invitations, greetings, and other designs, you click Actions on the menu bar, point to New Mail Message Using, and then click the More Stationery command to open a dialog box with stationery options. Previously selected stationeries will appear below the More Stationery command. You also can create your own stationery. Stationery uses HTML message format, so recipients whose e-mail programs don't read HTML e-mail won't see the stationery, but they will still be able to read the text.

Creating an E-mail Message

An e-mail message looks similar to a memo, with header lines for Date, To, From, Cc, and Subject, followed by the body of the message. Outlook fills in the Date line with the date on which you send the message and the From line with your name or e-mail address; these lines are not visible in the window in which you create your e-mail message. You complete the other lines. The To line lists the e-mail addresses of one or more recipients. The Cc line lists the e-mail addresses of anyone who will receive a courtesy copy of the message. An optional Bcc line lists the e-mail addresses of anyone who will receive a blind courtesy copy of the message; the Bcc recipients are not visible to each other or to the To and Cc recipients. The Subject line provides a quick overview of the message topic, similar to a headline. The main part of the e-mail is the message body.

E-mail, like other types of communication, is governed by its own customs of behavior, called **netiquette** (short for Internet etiquette), which helps prevent miscommunication. As you write and send e-mail messages, keep in mind the following guidelines:

- **Think before you send.** Your words can have a lasting impact. Be sure your messages convey the thoughts you intend and want others to attribute to you. Your name and e-mail address are attached to every message that you send, and your message can be forwarded swiftly to others.
- **Be concise.** The recipient should be able to read and understand your message quickly.
- **Use standard capitalization.** Excessive use of uppercase is considered shouting, and exclusive use of lowercase is incorrect; both are difficult to read.
- **Check spelling and grammar.** Create and maintain a professional image by using standard spelling and grammar. What you say is just as important as how you say it.

- **Avoid sarcasm.** Without your vocal intonations and body language, a recipient may read your words with emotions or feelings you didn't intend. You can use punctuation marks and other characters to create **emoticons**—also called **smileys**—such as :-), to convey the intent of your words. (Tilt your head to the left to look at the emoticon sideways to see the "face"—in this case, a smile.) To learn additional emoticons, search the Web for emoticon or smiley dictionaries.
- **Don't send confidential information.** E-mail is not private; once you send a message, you lose control over where it may go and who might read it. Also, employers and schools usually can legally access their employees' and students' e-mail messages, even after a message is deleted from an Inbox.

Creating an E-mail Message

Reference Window

- Click the New Mail Message button on the Standard toolbar.
- Type recipient e-mail address(es) in the To text box (separate by semicolons).
- Type recipient e-mail address(es) in the Cc text box and the Bcc text box, as needed.
- Type a topic in the Subject text box, and then type the message body.
- Format the message as needed.
- Click the Send button.

You'll create an e-mail message. Although you would usually send messages to other people, you will send messages to yourself in this tutorial so you can practice sending and receiving messages.

To create an e-mail message:

1. Click the **New** button list arrow on the Standard toolbar. A list of new items you can create in Outlook appears. Because a Mail folder is the current folder, Mail Message appears at the top of the list, and is the default if you simply click the New button.

2. Click a blank area of the window to close the New button list, and then position the mouse pointer over the **New** button on the Standard toolbar. A ScreenTip appears identifying this button as the New Mail Message button. Notice that the icon next to the word New on the button is an open envelope and a piece of paper.

3. Click the **New** button on the Standard toolbar. A new Message window opens in Word with the blinking insertion point in the To text box. Your signature appears in the **message body**, where the content of your message appears; you'll type your message above the signature. Notice that the title bar indicates that this is an Untitled Message.

4. Type your e-mail address in the To text box. You could send the e-mail to multiple recipients by typing a semicolon between each address.

5. Press the **Tab** key twice to move to the Subject text box. You skipped the Cc text box because you aren't sending a courtesy copy of this e-mail to anyone.

   Trouble? If the insertion point is not in the Subject text box, then the Bcc text box is displayed. Press the Tab key again to move to the Subject text box, and then continue with Step 6.

6. Type **Peach Order** in the Subject text box, and then press the **Tab** key to move to the message body, just above the signature. As soon as you move the insertion point out of the Subject text box, the name in the title bar changes to match the contents of the Subject text box.

7. Type **Your peaches are a big hit with The Express Lane customers. Please double our order for the next three weeks.**, press the **Enter** key twice, and then type **Thank you.** (including the period).

You don't need to type your name because you included it as part of the signature. Before sending your message, however, you want to add some text formatting. You set up Outlook to use Word as your e-mail editor, which means that you have access to all the formatting features available in Word. For example, you can set bold, underline, and italics; change the font, font size, and font color; align and indent text; create a bulleted or numbered list; and even apply paragraph styles. People whose e-mail programs can't read formatted e-mail will still be able to read your messages in plain text.

To format text in an e-mail message:

1. Select the text **a big hit** in the message body. You'll make this text bold and orange.
2. Click the **Bold** button **B** on the Formatting toolbar.
3. Click the **Font Color** button list arrow **A ·** on the Formatting toolbar, and then click the **Orange** tile in the second column, second row of the palette that opens.
4. Press the **Down Arrow** key to deselect the text and move the insertion point to the next line. The text is reformatted.

You could add more formatting, but a little goes a long way. Try to be judicious in your use of text formatting. Use it to enhance your message rather than overwhelm it.

Setting the Importance and Sensitivity Levels

You can add icons that appear in the message pane of the Inbox to provide clues to the recipient about the importance and sensitivity of the message. You can specify an importance level of High ! or Low ↓ or leave the message set at the default Normal importance level. High importance tells the recipient that the message needs prompt attention, whereas a Low importance tells the recipient that the message can wait for a response. Use the importance level appropriately. If you send all messages with a High importance, recipients will learn to disregard the status.

You'll change the message importance level to high.

To change a message importance level:

1. Click the **Importance: High** button ! on the Standard toolbar. The button remains selected as an indicator of the message's importance level. See Figure 1-6.

Figure 1-6	Completed e-mail message

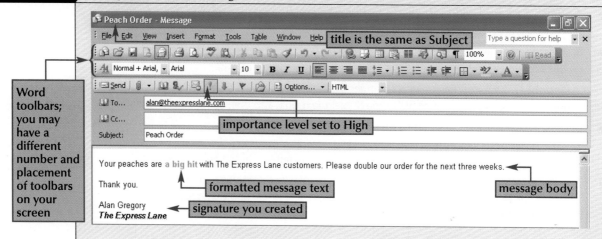

Word toolbars; you may have a different number and placement of toolbars on your screen

You can also change the normal sensitivity level for the message to Personal, Private, or Confidential. This is another way to help recipients determine the content of a message before reading it. To set the sensitivity level, click the Options button on the Standard tool-bar in the Message window, click the Sensitivity list arrow in the Options dialog box, and then select the sensitivity level you want for the message. You'll leave the sensitivity set to Normal for this message.

Sending E-mail

There are a variety of ways you can set up Outlook for sending messages. Your messages can be sent immediately (assuming your computer is connected to your e-mail server), or you can set it up so messages remain in the Outbox until you click the Send/Receive but-ton. You also can set up a schedule, where Outlook automatically sends and receives mes-sages at regular intervals that you specify (such as every five minutes or every few hours).

If you are working **offline** (not connected to your e-mail server) or if you have a dial-up connection, any messages you write remain in the Outbox until you choose to send them. You select how messages are sent in the Options dialog box. You'll set these options now.

To change your message delivery options:

► 1. Click the **Inbox - Microsoft Outlook** button on the taskbar to return to the Inbox.

► 2. Click **Tools** on the menu bar, click **Options** to open the Options dialog box, and then click the **Mail Setup** tab.

► 3. In the Send/Receive section, click the **Send immediately when connected** check box to remove the check mark, if necessary. Now Outlook will move your completed messages into the Outbox until you choose to send them rather than immediately sending them to your e-mail server.

► 4. Click the **OK** button.

When you click the Send button in the Message window, the message will move to the Outbox. You must then click the Send/Receive button on the Standard toolbar to check for and deliver new messages.

To send a message to the Outbox:

► 1. Click the **Peach Order - Message** button on the taskbar to return to your message.

► 2. Click the **Send** button on the message toolbar. The Message window closes and the mes-sage moves to the Outbox. You are returned to the Outlook window.

The Outbox folder name in the Mail pane changes to boldface and is followed by [1], which indicates that there is one outgoing message. You can send and receive e-mail from any folder in the Mail pane; you'll switch to the Outbox to deliver this message.

To switch to the Outbox and send the message:

► 1. Click **Outbox** in the Folder List pane. The message in the Outbox folder appears in the Outbox main window. See Figure 1-7.

| Figure 1-7 | Message in Outbox |

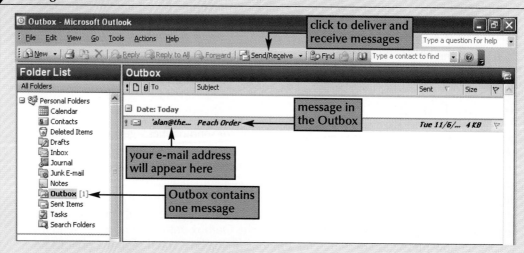

2. Click the **Send/Receive** button on the Standard toolbar to send the message. The Outlook Send/Receive Progress dialog box remains open until the message is sent. After the message is sent, the Outbox is empty and the boldface and [1] have disappeared.

Trouble? If you are not already connected to the Internet, connect now.

Trouble? If Outlook requests a password, you need to enter your password before you can send and receive your messages. Type your password, and then click the OK button.

A copy of the message is stored in the Sent Items folder, which provides a record of all the messages you sent. The time your e-mail takes to arrive at its destination will vary, depending on the size of the message, the speed of your Internet connection, and the number of other users on the Internet.

While sending your outgoing messages, Outlook may check your mail server for messages you have received since you last checked. If you have messages, they will be delivered to your Inbox. The message you just sent to yourself might appear in your Inbox instantly, and you might receive other messages to you that are unrelated to this tutorial.

Organizing Contact Information

The Contacts folder is an address book where you store information about the people and businesses with whom you communicate. Each person or organization is called a **contact**. You can store business-related information about each contact, including job title, phone and fax numbers, postal and Web addresses, and e-mail addresses, as well as more personal information, such as birthdays, anniversaries, and spouse and children's names.

Each piece of information you enter about a contact is called a **field**. For example, a complete contact name, such as Mr. Salvador F. Aiello, Jr., is comprised of a Title field, First field, Middle field, Last field, and Suffix field. The field's name or label identifies what information is stored in that field. You can use fields to sort, group, or look up contacts by any part of the name.

Creating Contacts

The Express Lane stores information about its suppliers and customers in the **Contacts** folder. Alan has asked you to create new contacts for several suppliers. You can start a new contact from any folder by clicking the New button list arrow on the Standard toolbar and then clicking New Contact. Instead, you'll switch to the Contacts folder.

To create a contact:

▶ 1. Click **Contacts** in the Folders List pane to display the Contacts folder. The icon on the New button changes to reflect the most likely item you'll want to create from this folder—in this case, a new contact.

▶ 2. Click the **New** button on the Standard toolbar. A new Contact window opens, displaying text boxes in which to enter the contact information.

▶ 3. Maximize the Contact window, if necessary.

Contact information is entered on two tabs. The General tab stores the most pertinent information about a contact, including the contact's name, job title and company, phone numbers, and addresses. The Details tab contains less frequently needed information, such as the names of the contact's manager, assistant, and spouse, as well as the contact's birthday, anniversary, and nickname.

Creating a Contact

Reference Window

- Click the New Contact button on the Standard toolbar to open a blank Contact window.
- Enter the contact's name, job title, company, mailing address, phone numbers, e-mail addresses, and Web site (click the down arrow to select other address, number, or e-mail options).
- Click the Details tab and enter other business or personal data as needed.
- Click the Save and New button on the Standard toolbar to create another contact (or click the Save and Close button if this is the last contact).
- If the Duplicate Contact Detected dialog box opens, select whether to add contact anyway or merge with existing contact, and then click the OK button.

You'll enter the first contact's name and company.

To enter a contact's name and company:

▶ 1. Type **Mr. Salvador F. Aiello, Jr.** in the Full Name text box, and then press the **Enter** key. The insertion point moves to the next text box (the Job title text box), and the contact name appears, last name first, in the File as text box. By default, Outlook organizes your contacts by their last names. The contact's name also appears in the title bar of the Contact window.

▶ 2. Click the **Full Name** button. The Check Full Name dialog box opens. Although you entered the contact name in one text box, Outlook stores each part of the name as a separate field. See Figure 1-8.

Figure 1-8 ▶ Check Full Name dialog box

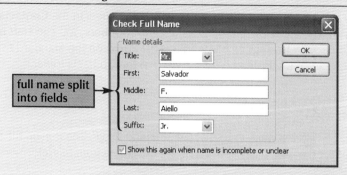

full name split into fields ▶

3. Click the **Cancel** button to close the dialog box without making any changes. If Outlook cannot tell how to distinguish part of a name, the Check Full Name dialog box will open so that you can correct the fields.

4. Click in the **Job title** text box, and then type **President**.

5. Press the **Tab** key to move to the Company text box, and then type **Green Grocer Produce**.

Next you'll enter the contact's phone numbers. You can enter as many as 19 numbers per contact. No matter how you enter the numbers—with or without spaces, hyphens, or parentheses—Outlook formats them consistently, such as (415) 555-3928.

To enter a contact's phone numbers, mailing address, and e-mail address:

1. Click in the **Business** text box in the Phone numbers section. Clicking the Business button opens the Check Phone Number dialog box, which is similar in function and appearance to the Check Full Name dialog box.

   Trouble? If the Location Information dialog box opens, enter the appropriate information about your location, and then click the OK button. If the Phone and Modem Options dialog box opens, click the Cancel button.

2. Type **415 555 9753**, and then press the **Tab** key. Outlook formats the phone number with parentheses around the area code and a hyphen after the prefix, even though you didn't type them.

   Next to each phone number text box is a down arrow button that you can click to change the name of the phone field. Although you can display only four phone fields at a time, you can enter information in all the fields, using one text box or all four text boxes.

3. Click the **down arrow** button 🔽 next to Home, click **Assistant** to change the field label, and then enter **415-555-9752** for the phone number of Salvador's assistant.

   You'll switch to the Details tab to enter the name of Salvador's assistant, and then return to the General tab to enter his fax number, postal address, and e-mail address.

4. Click the **Details** tab, click in the Assistant's name text box, and then type **Cynthia Lopez**.

5. Click the **General** tab, and then enter **415-555-6441** as the Business Fax number.

6. Click in the **Business** text box in the Addresses section, type **12 Haymarket Blvd.**, press the **Enter** key, and then type **San Francisco, CA 94102**. You could verify that Outlook recorded the address in the correct fields by clicking the Business button, but you don't need to do so for a simple address.

As soon as you started typing the address, the This is the mailing address check box becomes checked. Outlook assumes that the first address you enter for a contact is the mailing address. You could enter additional addresses and specify any one of them as the mailing address.

7. Click in the **E-mail** text box, type your own e-mail address, and then click in the Display as text box. The e-mail address you typed becomes underlined, and the contact's name appears in the Display as text box with your e-mail in parentheses after the name. The Display as text box shows how the e-mail address will appear in the To text box of e-mail messages. You'll change the Display as text to the contact's name.

8. Select all the text in the Display as text box (including your e-mail address), and then type **Sal Aiello**. See Figure 1-9.

Completed Contact window for Salvador F. Aiello Jr. ◄ **Figure 1-9**

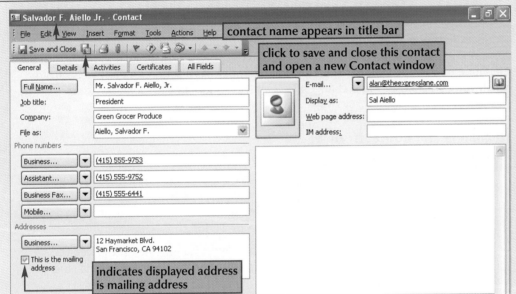

In most cases, each contact would have a unique e-mail address to which you would send e-mail messages. You have completed the contact information for Salvador. You can close his Contact window and open a new Contact window in the same step.

To create additional contacts:

1. Click the **Save and New** button 🖫 on the Standard toolbar to save Salvador's contact information and open a new Contact window.

2. Enter the following information: full name **Julia Shang**, job title **Manager**, company **Foods Naturally**, business phone **415-555-1224**, business fax **415-555-4331**, and business address **19 Hillcrest Way, Novato, CA 94132**. Use your own e-mail address, but display as **Julia Shang**.

3. Click the **Save and New** button 🖫 on the Standard toolbar. Outlook detects that another contact already has the same e-mail address as Julia Shang and opens the Duplicate Contact Detected dialog box. Click the **Add this as a new contact anyway** option button, and then click the **OK** button.

4. Enter the following contact information: full name **Kelley Ming**, company **Ming Nuts Company**, business phone **415-555-9797**, and business address **2932 Post Street, San Francisco, CA 94110**. Use your own e-mail address, but display as **Kelley Ming**.

5. Click the **Save and New** button 🖫 on the Standard toolbar, add Kelley Ming as a new contact anyway, and then enter the following contact information: full name **Alan Gregory** and company **The Express Lane**; use your e-mail address, but display as **Alan Gregory**.

6. Click the **Save and Close** button on the Standard toolbar and add Alan Gregory as a new contact anyway to save his contact information and return to the Contacts folder. The four contacts you added appear in the Contacts main window, sorted alphabetically by last name.

All of the information about a contact is called a **contact card**. There are a variety of ways to look at the information in the Contacts folder. **Views** specify how information in a folder is organized and which details are visible. Address Cards view displays names and addresses in blocks. Detailed Address Cards view displays additional information in this same format. Phone List view displays details about your contacts, such as name, job title, telephone numbers, in columns. Each Outlook folder has a set of standard views from which you can choose. You'll change the Contacts folder view to Detailed Address Cards.

To change the Contacts view:

1. Click the **Contacts** button in the Navigation Pane. The My Contacts pane appears at the top of the Navigation Pane with the Contacts folder listed. The Current View pane appears below the My Contacts pane, and it lists all the available standard views for the Contacts folder. The default is Address Cards, which displays each contact's name, mailing address, up to four phone numbers, and the contact's e-mail address.

2. Click the **Detailed Address Cards** option button in the Current View pane. Detailed Address Cards view displays more contact information in the main window than the Address Cards view. See Figure 1-10.

Contacts in Detailed Address Cards view | **Figure 1-10**

In the Address Cards and Detailed Address Cards views, Outlook organizes your contacts in the main window in alphabetical order by last name, as specified in the File as text box. When you have many contacts, you find a certain contact quickly by clicking the letter button along the right side of the main window that corresponds to the first letter of a contact's last name. Then use the scroll bar at the bottom of the window to display that contact.

Editing Contacts

Many aspects of a contact's information may change over time. A person or company may move to a new street address or be assigned a new area code. A person may change jobs periodically. You may discover that you entered information incorrectly. Rather than deleting the card and starting over, you can update the existing contact card as needed. Simply double-click the contact to open its Contact window, and edit the information as needed. You can also make the change directly in the Contacts folder from the Address Cards or Detailed Address Cards view.

Alan tells you that the ZIP code for Foods Naturally is actually 94947. You'll make this correction directly in the Detailed Address Cards view.

To edit a contact:

▶ **1.** Click the letter **S** along the right side of the Contacts main window to select Julia Shang's contact card.

> **Trouble?** If your contacts list has additional contacts, the first contact beginning with "s" will be selected. Scroll until you can see Julia Shang's contact card.

▶ **2.** Click the address portion of Julia Shang's contact card to position the insertion point anywhere within the address.

▶ **3.** Use the arrow keys to move the insertion point between the 4 and 1 in the ZIP code.

▶ **4.** Type **947**, and then press the **Delete** key three times to erase the incorrect digits.

▶ **5.** Click anywhere outside Julia Shang's contact card. Outlook saves the changes.

No matter how many changes you need to make to a contact's information, the contact card remains neat and organized.

Sending Contact Information by E-mail

If you ever need to send some of your contacts to others, you can do so quickly by forwarding the contact information. When you forward contact information as an Outlook contact card, it includes the same data contained in your Contacts folder. If you forward the Outlook contact card, the recipient must use Outlook in order to be able to read the card. Not only are you sending the most complete information, but the recipient can also quickly drag the contact into his or her own Contacts folder. To forward a contact card, right-click the contact card in the Contacts folder, and then click Forward Items on the shortcut menu. A new Message window opens with the contact card as an attachment to the message.

If you are not sure if the recipient uses Outlook, you can send contact information as a vCard. A **vCard** is a file that contains a contact's personal information, such as the contacts name, mailing address, phone numbers, and e-mail address. The vCard files are compatible with other popular communication and information management programs. You can also use vCards to exchange contact information with handheld personal digital assistants (PDAs). To send a contact card as a vCard, click the contact card in the Contacts folder to select it, click Actions on the menu bar, and then click Forward as vCard. A new Message window opens with the vCard included as an attachment.

When you receive a forwarded contact card, you can add the contact information directly to your Contacts folder without retyping the information. Just drag the contact card from the message to the Contacts folder, and the new contact card is created.

Creating and Modifying Distribution Lists

Sometimes you'll find that you repeatedly send on e-mail message—such as a weekly progress report or company updates—to the same group of people. Rather than selecting the names one by one from the Contacts list, you can create a distribution list. A **distribution list** is a group of people to whom you frequently send the same messages, such as all suppliers. A distribution list saves time and insures that you don't inadvertently leave out someone. You can create multiple distribution lists to meet you needs, and individuals can be included in more than one distribution list.

Creating a Distribution List

- Click the New button list arrow on the Standard toolbar, and then click Distribution List.
- Click the Select Members button near the top of the Distribution List window.
- Click the Show names from the list arrow, and then click Contacts.
- Double-click the names you want to add to the distribution list, and then click the OK button.
- Click in the Name text box, and then type a contact name for the distribution list.
- Click the Save and Close button on the Standard toolbar.

Alan asks you to create a distribution list to all The Express Lane suppliers as he frequently needs to send the same information to all of them.

To create a distribution list:

1. Click the **New** button list arrow on the Standard toolbar, and then click **Distribution List**. A new Distribution List window opens.

2. Type **Suppliers** in the Name text box. This is the contact name for the distribution list.

3. Click the **Select Members** button below the Name text box. The Select Members dialog box opens.

4. If necessary, click the **Show Names from the** list arrow, and then click **Contacts**. A contact appears in the list box once for each e-mail address and fax number.

   You'll move the three suppliers into the distribution list.

5. Double-click the top **Julia Shang** entry to move the contact to the Add to distribution list box. Double-clicking the name is the same as clicking the name and then clicking the Members button.

6. Double-click the **Kelley Ming** entry and the top **Salvador F. Aiello Jr.** entry to select them as members of distribution list. See Figure 1-11.

Figure 1-11

Figure 1-11 — Select Members dialog box

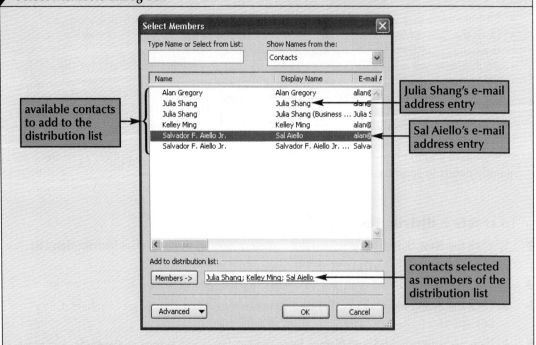

7. Click the **OK** button. The three suppliers appear as members of the Suppliers distribution list. See Figure 1-12.

Figure 1-12 — Distribution List window for the Suppliers distribution list

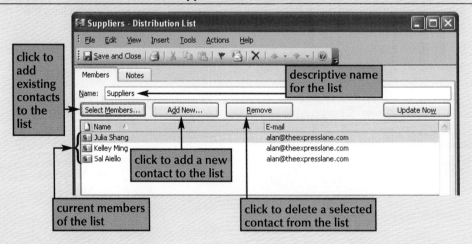

8. Click the **Save and Close** button on the Standard toolbar in the Distribution List window. The list appears in the Contacts folder filed under the name of the distribution list, Suppliers. A group icon in the upper-right corner of the contact card indicates that this is a distribution list rather than a one-person contact.

You can use the Suppliers distribution list contact just as you would any one-person contact.

Modifying a Distribution List

At times, you'll need to update a distribution list. You may need to delete a contact from the distribution list or add a new contact to the distribution list. You do this by double-clicking the distribution list contact in the Contacts folder to open its Distribution List window, and then click the Select Members button to add other contacts to the list or click the Remove button to delete a selected contact from the list. Removing a contact from a distribution list only deletes the contact from the distribution list; the individual's contact card remains intact in the Contacts folder. If you need to update the information for an existing contact, you would do so in the individual's contact card. If you find that you no longer need a distribution list, you delete it just like an individual contact.

Session 1.1 Quick Check

Review

1. Describe the purposes of the Inbox and the Outbox.
2. Define e-mail and list two benefits of using it.
3. What is a signature?
4. List five types of contact information that you can store in Outlook.
5. Explain the purpose of a distribution list.

Session 1.2

Receiving E-mail

You check for new e-mail messages by clicking the Send/Receive button on the Standard toolbar. Outlook connects to your e-mail server, if necessary, sends any messages in the Outbox, and receives any incoming messages that have arrived since you last checked. New messages are delivered into the Inbox.

You'll switch to the Inbox and download the message you sent yourself earlier.

To receive e-mail:

1. If you took a break after the previous session, make sure Outlook is running.

2. Click the **Mail** button in the Navigation Pane, and then click **Inbox** in the Favorite Folders pane.

3. Click the **Send/Receive** button on the Standard toolbar.

   Trouble? If you are not already connected to the Internet, connect now.

4. Watch for the new message to appear in the Inbox. The number of new messages you receive appears within parentheses next to the Inbox folder name in the Navigation Pane. See Figure 1-13. Your Inbox might contain additional e-mail messages.

Figure 1-13 ▶ **Received message in Inbox**

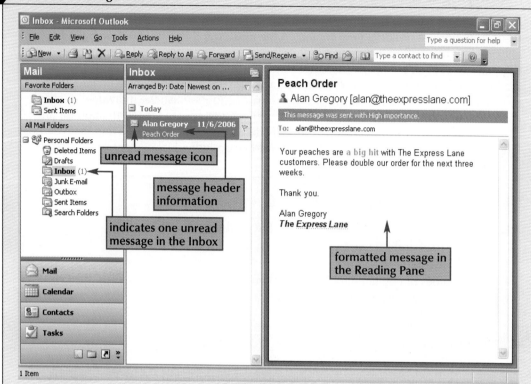

Trouble? If no messages appear, your e-mail server might not have received the message yet. Wait a few minutes, and then repeat Steps 3 and 4.

Once a message arrives, you can read it. The Inbox folder is divided into two panes. The Inbox main window displays a list of all e-mail messages that you have received, along with information about the message. The **message header** includes the sender's name, the message subject, and the date the message was received, as well as icons that indicate the message's status (such as the message's importance level and whether the message has been read). The **Reading Pane** displays the content of the selected message in a memo format. The subject, the sender, importance level, and all the recipients (except Bcc recipients) appear at the top of the memo. You can resize the panes by dragging the border between the Inbox main window and the Reading Pane left or right.

To read a message:

▶ 1. Click the **Peach Order** message in the Inbox main window to display its contents in the Reading Pane. In a moment, the mail icon changes from unread ✉ to read ✉, and the message no longer appears in boldface.

   Trouble? If the Reading Pane does not appear on your screen or if it appears on the bottom of the screen, click View on the menu bar, point to Reading Pane, and then click Right.

   Trouble? If the mail icon in the Inbox main window does not change to indicate that the message has been read, click Tools on the menu bar, click Options, click the Other tab, click the Reading Pane button, click the Mark items as read when viewed in the Reading Pane check box to select it, and then click the OK button twice.

2. Read the message in the Reading Pane. Because Outlook can view HTML messages, the formatting added to the message is visible.

Trouble? If you don't see the HTML formatting, your mail server may not display the HTML formatting in e-mail messages. Continue with the tutorial.

You can also open a message in its own window by double-clicking the message header in the Inbox pane. After you read a message, you have several options—you can leave the message in the Inbox and deal with it later, reply to the message, forward the message to others, print it, file it, or delete it.

Replying to and Forwarding Messages

Many messages you receive require some sort of response—for example, confirmation you received the information, the answer to a question, or sending the message to another person. The quickest way to respond to messages is to use the Reply, Reply to All, and Forward features. The **Reply** feature responds to the sender, and the **Reply to All** feature responds to the sender and all recipients (including any Bcc recipients); Outlook inserts the e-mail addresses into the appropriate text boxes. The **Forward** feature sends a copy of the message to one or more recipients you specify; you enter the e-mail addresses in the To or Cc text box. With both the Reply and Forward features, the original message is included for reference, separated from your new message by a line and the original message header information. By default, any new text you type is added at the top of the message body, above the original message. This makes it simpler for recipients to read your message because they don't have to scroll through the original message text to find the new text.

You'll reply to the Peach Order message. In reality, you would respond to someone other than yourself.

To reply to a message:

1. Make sure that the **Peach Order** message is selected in the Inbox main window, and then click the **Reply** button on the Standard toolbar. A Message window opens with the receiver's name and e-mail address in the To text box (in this case, your name and address) and RE: (short for Regarding) inserted at the beginning of the Subject line. The body of the original message appears in the message body pane below a divider line, and the insertion point is blinking above the message, ready for you to type your reply.

2. If necessary, click in the message area, and then type **You will receive double shipments of peaches for the next three weeks. Thank you for your order.**, press the **Enter** key twice, and then type your name (remember that your signature is not added for replies). Your reply message appears in blue because you selected HTML format.

Trouble? Depending on how your computer is configured, you might not see the HTML formatting.

3. Click the **Send** button on the message toolbar to move the message to the Outbox. The icon next to the message header in the Inbox main window changes to 🔄 to indicate that this message has been replied to.

Next you'll forward the message to Julia Shang, the manager at Foods Naturally. Because Julia's contact information is in the Contacts folder, you can address the message to her quickly.

To forward a message:

1. Make sure that the **Peach Order** message is selected in the Inbox main window, and then click the **Forward** button on the Standard toolbar. This time, the insertion point is in the empty To text box and FW: (for Forward) precedes the Subject line.

2. Type **Julia Shang** in the To text box, and then press the **Tab** key. A wavy red line appears below the name, indicating that multiple contact information is available for that contact.

3. Right-click **Julia Shang**, and then click **Julia Shang**, the entry with her e-mail address (do not click the Julia Shang (Business Fax) entry). When Outlook recognizes the contact name as an item in the Contacts folder with a valid e-mail address, it underlines it.

4. Click at the top of the message body, above the forwarded message, and then type **Please update The Express Lane account.**

5. Click the **Send** button on the message toolbar to move the message to the Outbox. The icon next to the message header in the Inbox main window changes to [icon] to indicate that this message has been forwarded.

6. Click the **Send/Receive** button on the Standard toolbar, if necessary, to send the messages to your mail server.

Alan asks you to print the message for future reference.

Printing Messages

Although e-mail eliminates the need for paper messages, sometimes you'll want a printed copy of a message to file or distribute, or to read when you're not at your computer. You can use the Print button on the Standard toolbar to print a selected message with the default settings, or you can use the Print command on the File menu to open the Print dialog box, where you can verify and change settings before you print. All default print styles include the print date, user name, and page number in the footer. You'll use the Print dialog box to verify the settings and then print the Peach Order message.

To verify settings and print a message:

1. If necessary, select the **Peach Order** message in the Inbox main window.

2. Click **File** on the menu bar, and then click **Print**. The Print dialog box opens.

3. Make sure that the correct printer appears in the Name list box.

   Trouble? If you're not sure which printer to use, ask your instructor or technical support person for assistance.

4. If necessary, click **Memo Style** in the Print style section to select it.

   Memo style prints the contents of the selected item—in this case, the e-mail message. Table Style prints the view of the selected folder—in this case, the Inbox folder. Other Outlook folders display different print style options.

5. Click the **OK** button. The message prints.

In your work at The Express Lane, you'll often want to send information that is stored in a variety of files on your computer. Some of this information could be typed into an e-mail message, but many kinds of files (such as photos and spreadsheets) can't be inserted into e-mail messages. Instead, you can send files as attachments.

Working with Attachments

An **attachment** is a file that you send with an e-mail message. Attachments can be any type of file, including documents (such as a Word document, Excel workbook, or PowerPoint slide presentation), images, sounds, and programs. For example, you might send an attachment containing The Express Lane's latest sales figures to Alan for his review. Recipients can then save and open the file; the recipient must have the original program or a program that can read that file type. For example, if Alan receives a Lotus 1-2-3 spreadsheet, he can open and save it with Excel.

To attach a file to an e-mail:

1. With the Inbox folder selected, click the **New** button on the Standard toolbar to open a new Message window.

2. Click the **To** button. The Select Names dialog box opens.

3. Click **Alan Gregory** in the list of contacts, and then click the **To** button at the bottom of the dialog box. Alan's name is added to the To list..

4. Click the **OK** button.

5. Type **Latest Sales** in the Subject text box.

6. In the message body area, type **The attached Excel workbook contains the latest sales figures. It looks like we're on track. Let me know if you have any comments.**

7. Click the **Insert File** button on the Standard toolbar. The Insert File dialog box opens; it functions like the Open dialog box.

8. Change the Look in list box to the **Tutorial.01\Tutorial** folder included with your Data Files.

   Trouble? If you don't have the Outlook Data Files, you need to get them before you can proceed. Your instructor will either give you the Data Files or ask you to obtain them from a specified location (such as a network drive). In either case, be sure that you make a backup copy of your Data Files before you start using them, so that the original files will be available on your copied disk in case you need to start over because of an error or problem. If you have any questions about the Data Files, see your instructor or technical support person for assistance.

9. Double-click **Sales** in the file list. The file is attached to your e-mail message, and the Insert File dialog box closes. See Figure 1-14. The message is ready to send.

Message with attached file   **Figure 1-14**

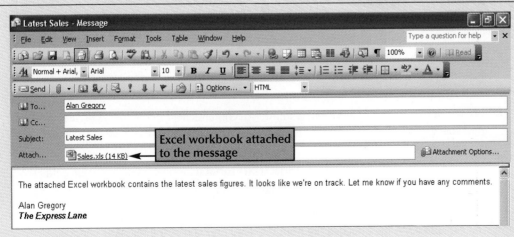

10. Click the **Send** button on the message toolbar, and then click the **Send/Receive** button on the Inbox Standard toolbar to send the message to your mail server and receive the two messages you sent earlier.

A message with an attachment may take a bit longer to send because it's larger than an e-mail message without an attachment. Messages with attached files display a paper clip icon in the message header. If the appropriate program is installed on your computer, you can open the attached file from the message itself. You can also save the attachment to your computer and then open, edit, and move it like any other file on your computer.

You can reply to or forward any message with an attachment, but the attachment is included only in the forwarded message because you will rarely, if ever, want to return the same file to the sender.

After you receive the message with the attachment, you'll save the attachment and then view it from within the message.

To save and view the message attachment:

1. If the Latest Sales message (with the attachment) is not already in your Inbox, click the **Send/Receive** button on the Standard toolbar. It might take a bit longer than usual to download the message with the attachment.

2. Click the **Latest Sales** message in the Inbox pane to view the message in the Reading Pane. The attachment icon appears below the date in the message header in the Inbox pane and the file icon and name appear in the Reading Pane. See Figure 1-15.

| Figure 1-15 | Message with attached file |

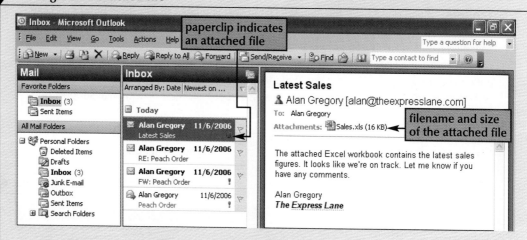

3. Double-click the **Latest Sales** message in the Inbox main window. The message opens in its own window. You can open and read messages this way if you don't want to use the Reading Pane.

4. Right-click the attached file **Sales.xls** in the Attachments field in the message header in the Message window, and then click **Save As** on the shortcut menu. The Save Attachment dialog box opens, where you can select the location to save the attachment.

5. Change the Save in list box to the **Tutorial.01\Tutorial** folder included with your Data Files.

6. Change the filename to **First Quarter Sales**, and then click the **Save** button to save the attached file. You can work with this file just as you would any other file on disk.

You can also open the attached file from the Reading Pane or the Message window.

7. Click the **Close** button ⊠ on the message window title bar, and then double-click **Sales.xls** in the Reading Pane. The Opening Mail Attachment dialog box opens, warning you that you should only open attachments from a trusted source.

    Trouble? If the Opening Mail Attachment dialog box doesn't open, skip the action in Step 8, but read the step anyway.

8. Click the **Open** button. The attached file opens in its associated program—in this case, Excel. You can read, edit, format, and save the file just as you would any other Excel workbook.

    Trouble? If the file opens in a spreadsheet program other than Excel, your computer might be configured to associate the file extension .xls with spreadsheet programs other than Excel. Continue with Step 9.

9. Review the sales figures, and then click the **Close** button ⊠ on the Excel window title bar to close the workbook and exit Excel.

    Trouble? If a dialog box opens asking whether you want to save changes, click the No button.

So far, all the messages you received are stored in the Inbox folder.

Flagging Messages

Some messages you receive require a specific response or action. Although the subject should be informative and the message can provide explicit instructions, often a more obvious reminder would better draw attention messages that require action. A **message flag** is an icon that appears in the message header. To better organize or prioritize your messages, you can choose from six flag colors. If you add a reminder, the message flag also includes text that appears in the Reading Pane or Message window and even a deadline. In the Flag for Follow Up dialog box, you can choose from preset flag text or enter your own text, and you can select a specific due date or enter descriptive words such as "tomorrow" that Outlook converts to the correct date. Outlook will then display a reminder about the flag at the appropriate time.

You can also add a flag with preset or custom text and a deadline to messages you send to others. You would click the Message Flag button on the Standard toolbar in the Message window to open the Flag for Follow Up dialog box, and select or enter the flag text and due date.

You'll add preset flag text with a deadline of tomorrow to the message to Julia Shang.

To flag a message:

1. Right-click the **flag** icon in the Latest Sales message header in the Inbox main window. The list of available flag colors appears on the shortcut menu.

2. Click **Green Flag** on the shortcut menu. The flag color changes to green in the Inbox pane and the Follow up banner appears above the message header in the Reading Pane.

3. Right-click the **flag** icon in the message header in the Inbox main window, and then click **Add Reminder**. The Flag for Follow Up dialog box opens. See Figure 1-16.

Figure 1-16 ▶ Flag for Follow Up dialog box

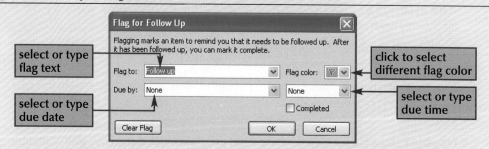

You want to set the flag message to Review and add a due date for tomorrow by 5 p.m.

▶ **4.** Click the **Flag to** list arrow to display the preset flag options, and then click **Review**.

▶ **5.** Click the left **Due by** list arrow to open a calendar showing this month with today's date highlighted, click the date three working days from now, click the right **Due by** list arrow, and then click **5:00 PM**.

▶ **6.** Click the **OK** button. The Flag for Follow Up dialog box closes. The Follow up banner in the Reading Pane changes to reflect the selections you made in the Flag for Follow Up dialog box. See Figure 1-17.

Figure 1-17 ▶ Message with flag

Once you have performed the requested action, you can mark the flag completed by clicking the flag icon in the message header until a check mark replaces the flag.

Organizing/Managing Messages

As you can readily see, messages can collect quickly in your Inbox. Even if you respond to each message as it arrives, all the original messages still remain in your Inbox. Some messages you'll want to file and store, just as you would file and store paper memos in a file cabinet. Other messages you'll want to delete.

Creating a Folder

The Folder List acts like an electronic file cabinet. You should create a logical folder structure in which to store your messages. For example, an employee of The Express Lane might create subfolders named "Customers" and "Suppliers" within the Inbox folder. You can create folders at the same level as the default folders, such as Inbox, Outbox, and Sent Messages, or you can create subfolders within these main folders. For now, you'll create one subfolder in the Inbox folder, named "Suppliers."

To create a folder in the Inbox folder:

1. Right-click the **Inbox** folder in the All Mail Folders pane, and then click **New Folder** on the shortcut menu. The Create New Folder dialog box opens.

2. Type **Suppliers** in the Name text box.

3. If necessary, click the **Folder contains** list arrow, and then click **Mail and Post Items**. You can also create subfolders to store contacts, notes, tasks, and so on.

4. Click **Inbox** in the Select where to place the folder list box if it's not already selected. See Figure 1-18.

Create New Folder dialog box ◄ **Figure 1-18**

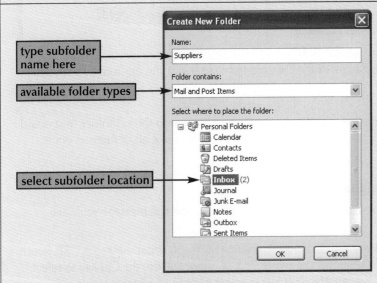

5. Click the **OK** button. The new folder appears indented under the Inbox folder in the All Mail Folders pane in the Navigation Pane.

Now you can file any messages related to The Express Lane in the new subfolder.

Filing Messages

As soon as you've dealt with a message in the Inbox, you should move it out of the Inbox; otherwise it will become cluttered, and you won't know which messages you've dealt with and which you haven't. To file a message, you can drag selected messages from one folder to another or use the Move to Folder button on the Standard toolbar.

To file messages:

1. Select the **Peach Order** message in the Inbox main window. It is the first message that you will move.

2. Drag the Peach Order message to the **Suppliers** subfolder in the All Mail Folders pane in the Navigation Pane, but do not release the mouse button. See Figure 1-19.

| Figure 1-19 | Filing a message |

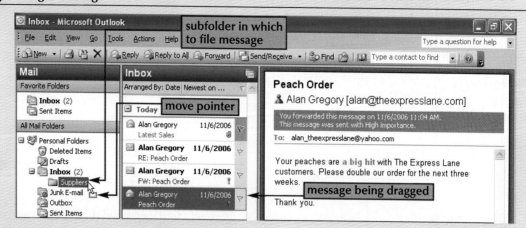

3. Release the mouse button to move the message from the Inbox into the Suppliers subfolder.

You want to move all messages related to The Express Lane into the subfolder. You could continue to move each message individually, but it's faster to move all of them at once.

To file multiple messages:

1. Click the **Latest Sales** message in the Inbox main window, the first message you want to file.

2. Press and hold the **Ctrl** key and click the remaining two Peach Order messages ("RE: Peach Order" and "FW: Peach Order") in the Inbox main window. You use the Ctrl key to select nonadjacent messages. You use the Shift key to select a range of adjacent messages.

3. Release the **Ctrl** key. The three messages are selected.

4. Drag the three selected messages from the Inbox main window into the **Suppliers** subfolder.

The Inbox is now empty of messages related to The Express Lane. However, the sales figures e-mail does not belong in the Suppliers folder. You'll create a new folder named "Sales" to file that e-mail.

To create another folder:

1. Right-click the **Inbox** main window title bar, and then click **New Folder**. The Create New Folder dialog box opens.

2. Type **Sales** in the Name text box, and then select **Mail and Post Items** in the Folder contains list box, if necessary.

3. Click **Inbox** in the Select where to place the folder list box if it's not already selected, and then click the **OK** button. The new folder appears indented under the Inbox folder in the All Mail Folders pane in the Navigation Pane.

You'll use a rule to move the sales figures message to the Sales folder.

Creating Rules

Rather than manually filing all your messages, you can create rules that specify how Outlook should process and organize them. For example, you can use rules to move messages to a folder based on their subjects, flag messages about a particular topic, or forward messages to a person or a distribution list.

Each **rule** includes three parts: the *conditions* that determine if a message is to be acted on, the *actions* that should be applied to qualifying messages, and any *exceptions* that remove a message from the qualifying group. For example, a rule might state that all messages you receive from Julia Shang (condition) are moved to the Suppliers folder (action) except for ones marked as High importance (exception). Outlook can apply rules to incoming, outgoing, or stored messages.

You can create a simple rule from common conditions and actions in the Create Rule dialog box, or use the Rules Wizard, a feature that steps you through the rule-writing process, to write more complex rules that also include exceptions. As you build a rule, you continue to refine the sentence that describes the conditions, actions, and exceptions.

If you are using Outlook with Exchange Server, you must be online to create rules.

Reference Window

Creating a Simple Rule

- Click the Create Rule button on the Standard toolbar.
- Select conditions and set their values as needed.
- Select actions and set their values as needed.
- Click the OK button.

You want to create a rule to move all sales messages related to the Sales folder. A message must be selected in order for the Create Rule button to be available. You can select any message to create a rule. Note that the information from the selected message automatically appears as conditions in the create Rule dialog box.

To create a rule:

1. Click the **Suppliers** folder in the Navigation Pane, and then click the **Latest Sales** message.

2. Click the **Create Rule** button 🖾 on the Standard toolbar. The Create Rule dialog box opens.

3. Click the **Subject contains** check box to insert a check mark. The Subject text box already contains the subject from the selected message, so you do not need to replace this text.

4. Click the **Move e-mail to folder** check box. The Rules and Alerts dialog box opens.

5. Click the **plus sign** button ⊞ next to Inbox in the Choose a folder list, click **Sales**, and then click the **OK** button. The conditions and actions for this rule are set. See Figure 1-20.

Figure 1-20

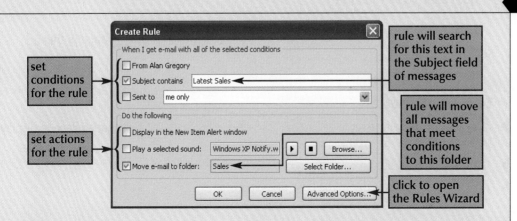

set conditions for the rule

set actions for the rule

rule will search for this text in the Subject field of messages

rule will move all messages that meet conditions to this folder

click to open the Rules Wizard

6. Click the **OK** button. The Success dialog box opens, indicating that the rule "Latest Sales" has been created. You want to run the rule on the message in the Inbox folder.

   Trouble? If a dialog box opens and displays the message, "This rule is a client-only rule, and will process only if Outlook is running," then you are set up to run Outlook with Exchange. This message appears because Outlook has determined that the rule requires access to your computer to run. Click the OK button. Outlook saves the rule and adds "(client only)" after the name of the rule in the Rules and Alerts dialog box to remind you that your computer must be logged onto Exchange for the rule to be run.

7. Click the **Run this rule now on messages already in the current folder** check box to select it, and then click the **OK** button.

   The rule runs on the messages in the Inbox folder and the Latest Sales message is moved to the Sales folder.

8. Click the **Sales** folder in the All Mail Folders in the Navigation Pane to confirm that the message was moved into this folder.

After you place messages in a variety of folders, you can further arrange them.

Rearranging Messages

As your folder structure becomes more complex and you have more stored messages, it might become difficult to locate a specific message you filed. Finding, using Search Folders, sorting, and changing views provide different ways to organize your messages.

Finding Messages

Rather than searching through multiple folders, you can have Outlook find the desired message. The Find command searches the From or Subject text boxes in a single folder for text that you specify. For searches of more than one criterion or multiple folders and sub-folders, you must use the Advanced Find feature.

Reference Window | **Finding Messages**

- Open the folder you want to search.
- Click the Find button on the Standard toolbar (*or* click Tools on the menu bar, and then click Find).
- Type the search text in the Look for text box.
- Select the folder to search in the Search In list box.
- Click the Find Now button.

You'll use the Find feature to look for replies to the peach order message in the Suppliers folder.

To find messages:

1. Click the **Suppliers** subfolder in the All Mail Folders pane in the Navigation Pane to display its contents in the main window.

2. Click the **Find** button on the Standard toolbar. The Find Bar opens.

3. Type **RE: Peach Order** in the Look for text box.

4. Make sure **Suppliers** appears in the Search In list box.

5. Click the **Find Now** button. After a moment, the one message that contains "RE: Peach Order" appears in the main window. See Figure 1-21.

Find results ◄ **Figure 1-21**

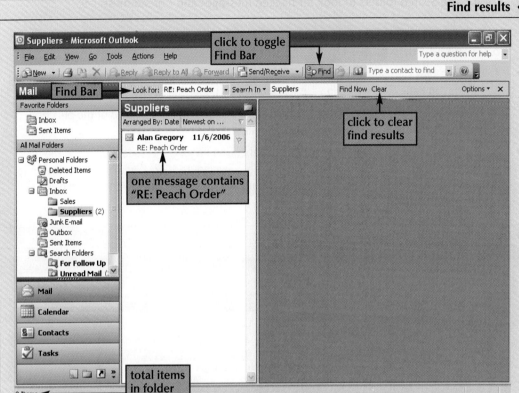

You could perform additional simple searches, but for now you're done.

6. Click the **Find** button on the Standard toolbar to close the Find Bar.

Once you close the Find Bar, all messages in that folder reappear. Another way to find specific messages is with Search Folders.

Using Search Folders

Search Folders are folders that display any e-mail messages that match specific search criteria. Any messages that meet the Search Folder's criteria are displayed in that Search Folder but remain stored in their current Outlook folders. This enables you to open one folder to view similar messages, but store them in other folders with a logical filing system. Outlook has several preset Search Folders. For example, the For Follow Up Search Folder displays any flagged messages you have stored, the Large Mail Search Folder displays any messages larger than 100 KB, and the Unread Mail Search Folder displays all messages that have an unread icon. A message can appear in more than one Search Folder. For example, a flagged message that is 200 KB and still marked as unread, will be displayed in at least three Search Folders: For Follow Up, Large Mail, and Unread Mail. You can use the existing Search Folders, customize them to better fit your needs, or create your own Search Folders.

If you delete a Search Folder, the messages that were displayed in that folder are not deleted because they are actually stored in other Outlook folders. However, if you delete an individual message from within a Search Folder, the message is also deleted from its storage folder.

You'll use Search folders to look for flagged messages and unread messages.

To view the For Follow Up Search Folder:

1. Click the **plus sign** button ⊞ next to Search Folders in the All Mail Folders pane in the Navigation Pane. The For Follow Up folder appears under the Search Folders folder.

   Trouble? If a minus sign button appears next to Search Folders instead of the plus sign button, the folder is already expanded. Skip to Step 2.

2. Click **For Follow Up** in the All Mail Folders pane. One flagged message appears in the main window under the group heading "Green Flag." See Figure 1-22. If you had more than one message flagged and used different flag colors, the messages would appear organized as different groups.

Figure 1-22	For Follow Up Search Folder

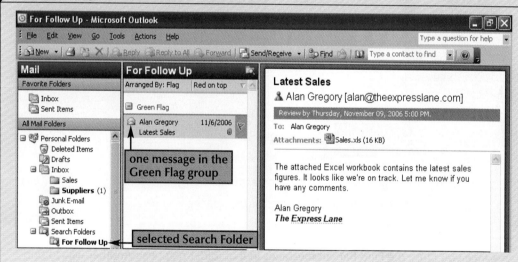

You'll use the New Search Folder dialog box to open the Unread Mail Search Folder. If you already have an Unread Mail folder in your Folder List, read, but do not complete the following set of steps.

To view the Unread Mail Search Folder:

1. Right-click **Search Folders** in the All Mail Folders pane in the Navigation pane, and then click **New Search Folder**. The New Search Folder dialog box opens. See Figure 1-23.

New Search Folder dialog box ◣ **Figure 1-23**

available preset Search Folders ➔

2. Click **Unread mail** in the Select a Search Folder list box, and then click the **OK** button. The contents of the Unread Mail Search Folder appears in the main window. The two messages you haven't yet read are listed. See Figure 1-24.

Unread Mail Search Folder ◣ **Figure 1-24**

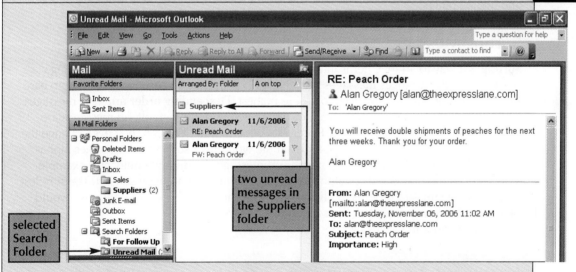

two unread messages in the Suppliers folder

selected Search Folder

Trouble? If you see fewer or more messages, you may have inadvertently changed a message icon from unread to read when moving it to the Suppliers folder or you may have received messages unrelated to this tutorial. Continue with the tutorial.

Another way to manage files is to change the view or arrangement.

Switching Views and Arrangements

There are a variety of ways to look at items in a folder. You are already familiar with views, which specify how items in a folder are organized and which details are visible. Each

Outlook folder has a set of standard views from which you can choose. **Arrangements** are a predefined arrangement of how items in a view are displayed. Views and arrangements enable you to see the same items in a folder in different ways.

To switch views and arrangements:

1. Click **Suppliers** in the All Mail Folders pane in the Navigation Pane to display the contents of this folder in the main window.

2. Click **View** on the menu bar, point to **Arrange By**, and then point to **Current View** to display the list of default views.

3. Click **Messages**. This is the default view, so the folder view in the main window probably didn't change. All the messages appear in the folder arranged according to the date they were received.

4. Click **View** on the menu bar, point to **Arrange By**, and then click **Conversation**. All the messages appear in the main window arranged according to their Subjects.

5. Click **View** on the menu bar, point to **Arrange By**, and then click **Importance**. All the messages appear in the main window arranged according to their importance levels, in this case High or none. Each level (High, Low, or none) becomes a heading for a different group. The other arrangements display the e-mail messages in different ways.

You could further customize a view by removing some of the existing column headings and adding others.

Sorting Messages

Sorting is a way to arrange items in a specific order—either ascending or descending. **Ascending order** arranges messages alphabetically from A to Z, chronologically from earliest to latest, or numerically from lowest to highest. **Descending order** arranges messages in reverse alphabetical, chronological, or numerical order. By default, all messages are sorted in descending order by their Received date and time. You can, however, change the field by which messages are sorted; for example, you might sort e-mail messages alphabetically by sender. Alternatively, you can sort messages by multiple fields; for example, you might sort e-mail messages alphabetically by sender and then by subject. The simplest way to change the sort order is to click a column heading in the folder pane. You would press the Shift key as you click the second sort column.

You'll sort your messages by importance level.

To sort messages by importance level:

1. Click the **High on top** column heading in the main window. The sort order changes to ascending by importance, as indicated by the up arrow icon in the column heading. See Figure 1-25.

Sorted messages ◄ Figure 1-25

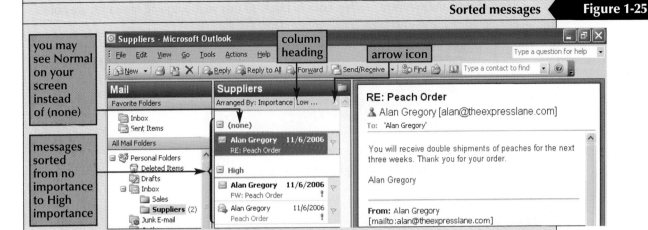

Trouble? If you don't see "on top" as part of the column heading, your main window is too narrow to display the entire column label. Click High to change the sort order to ascending by importance.

Trouble? If there is no High on top column heading, only one labeled Low on top, and the arrow icon points up, then the sort order is already ascending. Skip to Step 2.

2. Click the **Low on top** column heading in the main window. The sort order returns to descending by importance, as indicated by the down arrow icon in the column heading.

3. Click **View** on the menu bar, point to **Arrange By**, and then click **Date**.

You can sort messages in any view except Message Timeline view. Another way to make certain messages stand out is to color them.

Coloring Messages

Sometimes you'll want messages that you send to a certain person or that you receive from a certain person to stand out from all the other messages. A simple way to do this is to create a rule to change the color of the message headers in the Inbox for those messages. You choose to change all messages to or from a particular person to a color you select. You can also select a color for any messages that are sent only to you. You can set up both these rules in the Organize pane, which also provides another way to move items from one Outlook folder to another and to switch views.

You'll use the Organize pane to set up the rule to change the color of messages from yourself to Red.

To change the color of messages:

1. Click **Tools** on the menu bar, and then click **Organize**. The Ways to Organize Suppliers pane opens.

2. Click the **Using Colors** link. The options for setting colors for specific messages appear in the pane. You'll use the first sentence.

3. If necessary, click the left list arrow, and then click **from**.

4. If necessary, select the text in the text box, and then type your name.

5. If necessary, click the right list arrow, and then click **Red**. The rule is complete.

6. Click the **Apply Color** button. The rule is applied to the messages in the current folder, and all the message headers in the Suppliers folder change to red.

You'll change the message headers back to black, so that your outgoing messages are not all colored red, and then close the Organize pane.

7. Click the right list arrow in the Ways to Organize Suppliers pane, click **Auto**, and then click the **Apply Color** button. All the message headers in the Suppliers folder return to the default black.

8. Click **Tools** on the menu bar, and then click **Organize**. The Ways to Organize Suppliers pane closes.

You can use different colors to highlight messages to or from different people at one time.

Storing Messages

After a time, you may not need immediate access to the messages you have compiled in the Outlook folders. You can store messages in other file formats or by archiving them.

Saving Messages

You can use the Save As command to save messages and other Outlook items in other file formats so that you can save them on your hard drive or floppy disks, as you save your other files, and then delete them from Outlook. You can open such messages with other programs. For example, you can save an e-mail message as a Text Only (.txt) file that most word processing programs can read. You can also save HTML messages as HTML (.htm) files to preserve their original formatting.

Reference Window | **Saving Messages in Another File Format**

- Select the message or messages you want to save in another format.
- Click File on the menu bar, and then click Save As.
- Change the Save in location.
- Enter a new filename as needed.
- Click the Save as type list arrow, and then select the file format you want.
- Click the Save button.

You'll save the original Peach Order message as a Text Only file.

To save a message in another format:

1. Click the **Peach Order** message in the main window to select it.

2. Click **File** on the menu bar, and then click **Save As**. The Save As dialog box opens, with the subject listed in the File name text box.

3. Change the Save in location to the **Tutorial.01\Tutorial** folder included with your Data Files.

4. Click the **Save as type** list arrow to display the file formats from which you can select.

   Trouble? If your message did not retain the HTML formatting, then the format options available are Text Only, Outlook Template, Outlook Message Format, and Outlook Message Format - Unicode. Continue with Step 5.

5. Click **Text Only** to select that file format.

6. Click the **Save** button. The message is saved as a text file.

You or others can now open the file in Word or any other program that can read text files. The process is the same for saving and viewing files in HTML.

Archiving Mail Messages

Eventually, even the messages in your subfolders can become too numerous to manage easily. More often than not, you don't need immediate access to the older messages. Rather than reviewing your filed messages and moving older ones to a storage file, you can archive them. When you **archive** a folder, you transfer messages or other items stored in a folder (such as an attachment in the e-mail folder) to a personal folder file when the items have reached the age you specify. A **personal folders file** is a special storage file with a .pst extension that contains folders, messages, forms, and files; it can be viewed only in Outlook. Outlook calculates the age of an e-mail message from the date the message was sent or received, whichever is later. The personal folders file format for Outlook 2003 has greater storage capacity than and is incompatible with earlier versions of Outlook. However, Outlook 2003 can create and view personal folders files in both formats.

When you create an archive, your existing folder structure from Outlook is recreated in the archive file and all the messages are moved from Outlook into the archive file. If you want to archive only a subfolder, the entire folder structure is still recreated in the archive file; however, only the messages from the selected subfolder are moved into the archive file. For example, if you archive the Suppliers folder, the archive file will include both the Inbox and the Suppliers subfolder, but only the messages in the Suppliers subfolder will be moved. Any messages in the Inbox remain in the Outlook Inbox. All folders remain in place within Outlook after archiving—even empty ones.

You can manually archive a folder at any time, such as when you finish a project or event. You specify which folders to archive, the age of items to archive, and the name and location of the archive file.

To manually archive a folder:

1. Click **File** on the menu bar, and then click **Archive**. The Archive dialog box opens. See Figure 1-26.

Archive dialog box | **Figure 1-26**

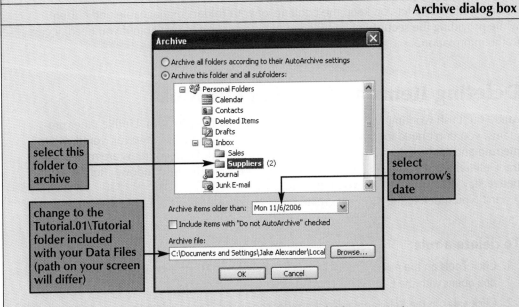

2. If necessary, click the **Archive this folder and all subfolders** option button.

3. If necessary, click the **plus sign** button ⊞ next to Inbox to display the subfolders, and then click the **Suppliers** folder.

4. Type **tomorrow** in the Archive items older than text box, and then press the **Tab** key. Outlook will move any files dated with today's date or earlier to the archive file.

5. Click the **Browse** button. The Open Personal Folders dialog box opens.

6. Change the Save in location to the **Tutorial.01\Tutorial** folder included with your Data Files, type **Suppliers Archive** as the filename, and then click the **OK** button.

7. Click the **OK** button in the Archive dialog box.

8. Click the **Yes** button to confirm that you want to archive all the items in the folder. All the messages in the Suppliers folder are moved into the archive file you specified. The empty Suppliers folder remains in the folder structure.

9. Repeat Steps 1 through 8 to create an archive for the **Sales** folder named **Sales Archive**.

The archived folders are open and displayed in the Folders List. You can access items in your archive files several ways: you can open the file using the Open command on the File menu and then drag the items you need to a current folder; you can add the archive file to your profile; or you can restore all the items in the archive file by using the Import and Export command on the File menu. If you don't need access to the archive folders, then you can close them.

To close archive folders:

1. Click the **Folder List** button 🗔 on the Navigation Pane, and then scroll down to see the two archive folders at the end of the list.

2. Right-click the top **Archive Folders** in the Folder List, and then click **Close "Archive Folders."** The folder closes.

3. Right-click the remaining **Archive Folders** in the Folder List, and then click **Close "Archive Folders."** The folder closes.

Archived folders let you keep the contents of your folders manageable and current while providing the security of knowing older information is available if you need access to the information.

Deleting Items and Exiting Outlook

After you finish working with Outlook, you should exit the program. Unlike other programs, you don't need to save or close any files. Before you exit, however, you'll delete the rule and each of the items you created in this tutorial. Deleted items are moved into the Deleted Items folder. This folder acts like the Recycle Bin in Windows. Items you delete stay in this folder until you empty it.

First, you'll delete the rule you created.

To delete a rule:

1. Click **Tools** on the menu bar, and then click **Rules and Alerts**. The Rules and Alerts dialog box opens with the E-mail Rules tab on top.

2. Click **sales** in the Rule (applied in the order shown) list box to select the rule, and then click the **Delete** button on the toolbar at the top of the tab.

3. Click the **Yes** button to confirm the deletion, and then click the **OK** button to close the Rules and Alerts dialog box. The rule is deleted.

Next, you'll delete the folders and e-mails you created.

To delete items:

▶ 1. Click the **Suppliers** folder in the All Folders pane in the Navigation Pane.

▶ 2. Click the **Delete** button ⊠ on the Standard toolbar, and then click the **Yes** button to confirm that the folder and all of its messages should be moved to the Deleted Items folder.

▶ 3. Click the **Sales** folder in the Folder List, click the **Delete** button ⊠ on the Standard toolbar, and then click the **Yes** button to confirm that the folder and all of its messages should be moved to the Deleted Items folder.

▶ 4. Switch to the **Sent Items** folder, click the first message you sent in this tutorial, press and hold the **Ctrl** key as you click each additional message you sent in this tutorial, release the **Ctrl** key, and then click the **Delete** button ⊠ on the Standard toolbar. The messages move to the Deleted Items folder.

▶ 5. Click the **Contacts** button in the Navigation Pane, press and hold the **Ctrl** key as you click each of the five contacts you created in this tutorial, release the **Ctrl** key, and then press the **Delete** key. The contacts you created for this tutorial are deleted.

▶ 6. Click the **plus sign** button ⊞ next to Search Folders in the Navigation pane, if necessary, click the **Unread Mail** folder, and then click the **Delete** button ⊠ on the Standard toolbar.

▶ 7. Right-click the **Deleted Items** folder in the All Folders pane, click **Empty "Deleted Items" Folder** on the shortcut menu, and then click the **Yes** button to confirm the deletion. The folder empties and the items are permanently deleted.

Finally you'll remove the signature you created and exit Outlook.

To delete a signature and exit Outlook:

▶ 1. Click **Tools** on the menu bar, click **Options**, and then click the **Mail Format** tab in the Options dialog box.

▶ 2. Click the **Signatures** button, click the name of your signature in the Signature list box, and then click the **Remove** button.

▶ 3. Click the **Yes** button to confirm that you want to delete this signature.

▶ 4. Click the **OK** button in the Create Signature dialog box, and then click the **OK** button in the Options dialog box. You're ready to exit Outlook.

▶ 5. Click the **Close** button ⊠ on the title bar to exit Outlook.

Alan thanks you for your help. The Express Lane can now fill all of its customers' orders for peaches until the end of the season. A happy customer means a profitable business.

Session 1.2 Quick Check

Review

1. Explain the difference between the Reply button and the Reply to All button.
2. True or False: You can save a file attached to a message, but you cannot open the attachment from within Outlook.
3. How do you move an e-mail message from the Inbox to a subfolder?
4. What is a Search Folder?
5. What is the purpose of a rule?
6. What does it mean to archive a folder?

Tutorial Summary

In this tutorial, you learned about the Outlook components, started Outlook, viewed its window elements, and navigated between components. You created and sent e-mail messages. You created and organized a contact list and created a distribution group. You received, read, replied to, forwarded, and printed e-mail messages. Then you added and read attachments to e-mail messages. You organized messages in subfolders by filing them manually and using a rule to move them. You rearranged messages by changing a folders view and arrangement, and sorting them. Finally, you saved messages in other formats, archived messages within a folder, and then deleted items you created.

Key Terms

archive	Folder Banner	Outlook Today
arrangement	Folder List	password
ascending order	Forward	personal folders file
attachment	host name	Reading Pane
Calendar	item	Reply
contact	Journal	Reply to All
contact card	Mail	Search Folder
Contacts	main window	rule
descending order	message flag	signature
distribution list	message header	smiley
e-mail	Microsoft Outlook	sorting
e-mail address	Navigation Pane	stationery template
emoticon	netiquette	Tasks
field	Notes	user ID
folder	offline	vCard
		view

Review Assignments

Data File needed for the Review Assignments: Tea.doc

Lora Shaw asks you to help her with customer communication for The Express Lane. Complete the following:

1. Create a signature that uses your name and "Customer Service Representative" as your title. Apply the signature to new messages and replies and forwards.
2. Create a new e-mail message addressed to your e-mail address with the subject "Welcome New Customer" and the message "Welcome to The Express Lane. We're sure you'll find our grocery delivery service more convenient and cheaper than your local grocery store—not to mention more healthful, because all our foods are certified organic. If you have any questions or comments, feel free to e-mail us."
3. Format the text of your e-mail in 12-point Times New Roman.
4. Send the e-mail to the Outbox and then to your mail server.
5. Create a contact card for Alan Gregory at The Express Lane with a fictional business mailing address and business phone number; use your own e-mail address.
6. Create a contact card for Lora based on Alan's contact card. Enter the same company information as on Alan Gregory's contact card. (*Hint:* To create a card with the business information entered automatically, select the contact card that contains the

business information you want to duplicate in the Contacts folder, click Actions on the menu bar, and then click New Contact from Same Company.) Type "Lora Shaw" in the Full Name text box. Type your e-mail address in the E-mail text box.

7. Create contact cards for the following three customers at their home addresses, using your e-mail address: (*Hint:* Click the down arrow button in the address section, and then click Home.)
   - Elliot Zander, 384 Leavenworth Street, San Francisco, CA 94103, 415-555-1232
   - Mai Ching, 1938 Grant Avenue, San Francisco, CA 94110, 415-555-0907
   - Lester Newhoun, 2938 Golden Gate Avenue, San Francisco, CA 94124, 415-555-6497

8. Create a distribution list named "Customers" that includes Mai Ching, Lester Newhoun, and Elliot Zander.

9. Edit Mai Ching's contact card to change the address to "1938 Presidio Street."

10. Create an e-mail message addressed to Lora Shaw. Type "Tea health benefits?" as the subject. Type "I've heard that drinking tea has health benefits. Do you have any information about this?" as the message body. Send the e-mail to the Outbox and then to your mail server.

11. Download your new messages. If the Tea health benefits? message hasn't arrived, wait a few minutes and try again.

12. Reply to the Tea health benefits? message with the text "In addition to being the world's second favorite drink to water, there is growing evidence of a link between tea and disease prevention, particularly cancer and heart disease. Check out our large selection of black, oolong, and green teas. The attached file has some information about teas. I hope this information is helpful."

13. Attach the **Tea** document located in the **Tutorial.01\Review** folder included with your Data Files to the file, and then send the message to your Outbox.

15. Forward the Tea health benefits? message to Alan Gregory with the message "Let's meet next week to talk about adding this information to our Web site." Mark it as high importance. Send the message to the Outbox.

16. Send all messages in your Outbox to your mail server.

17. Create a Mail and Post Items subfolder named "Customers" located within the Inbox.

18. Create a rule to move messages you receive from yourself to the Customers folder. Run the rule now.

19. Download your messages, and verify that the Welcome New Customer message and the three Tea health benefits? messages were filed in the Customers subfolder.

20. Add a blue flag to the Tea health benefits? message.

21. Find the messages in the Customers folder that contain the word "customer."

22. Save each of the messages that were found in HTML format to the **Tutorial.01\Review** folder included with your Data Files (if your server does not support HTML, then save the messages in Text Only format). Close the Find bar.

23. Create a new Mail flagged for follow up Search Folder, and then open the new folder.

24. Save the attachment in the RE: Tea health benefits? message as **Tea Health Benefits** in the **Tutorial.01\Review** folder included with your Data Files.

25. Print the RE: Tea health benefits? message and its attachment. (*Hint:* In the Print dialog box, select the Print attached files check box.)

26. Archive all the messages in the Customers folder to the **Tutorial.01\Review** folder included with your Data Files, using the filename **Customers Archive**. Close the archive folder.

27. Delete each Outlook item you created, including the Search Folder you created named for Follow Up1, the signature, the rule, the subfolder, the messages in the Sent Items folder, and the contacts, and then empty the Deleted Items folder.

Case Problem 1

Data File needed for this Case Problem: Amendments.doc

Answers Anytime   Answers Anytime is a unique tutoring service where students can e-mail specific questions and problem areas to subject experts and receive quick answers. The subject experts reply to students within two hours, either by e-mail message or e-mail message with an attachment. Complete the following:

1. Create a new e-mail message to your e-mail address with the subject "History questions" and the message "Please send information about the following: What is the Bill of Rights? When did women receive the right to vote? How does Rachel Carson fit into the environmental movement?" Press the Enter key after each question to place it on its own line, and then format the questions as a numbered list. Type your name at the end of the message. Send the message.

2. Create a contact card for Benji Tanago, Environmental History Expert, Answers Anytime, Pallas Road, Cincinnati, OH 45230, 513-555-6582, and your e-mail address.

3. Download your message, and then reply to the message using the following text formatted as a numbered list:

   1. See the attached document for information about the Bill of Rights.

   2. On August 26, 1920, Tennessee delivered the last needed vote and the Nineteenth Amendment was added to the Constitution. It states that "the right of citizens of the United States to vote shall not be denied by the United States or by any State on account of sex."

   3. I've forwarded this question to Benji Tanago, our resident expert on the environmental movement.

4. Attach the **Amendments** document located in the **Tutorial.01\Cases** folder included with your Data Files to the e-mail. Send the message to the Outbox.

5. Rather than retype Benji's information, you can send the contact card you just created. Switch to the Contacts folder, click Benji's contact card to select it, click Actions on the menu bar, and then click Forward as vCard. A Message window opens with the contact card included as an attachment. Enter your e-mail address in the To text box, and then send the message to the Outbox.

6. Forward the student's original message to Benji with a High importance level. Add the text "Hi, Benji. Question 3 is yours. Thanks."

7. Because you want to make sure that Benji responds in a timely manner, you want to recall the message if Benji hasn't read it within one week. Click the Options button on the toolbar in the message window, click the Expires after check box to insert a check mark, enter the date of one week from today, and then click the Close button. This option makes the message unavailable after the date you specified.

8. Send the message to the Outbox, and then send all the messages to your mail server.

9. Create a Mail and Post Items subfolder named "Answers" located in the Inbox.

10. Download your messages, and then find all messages in the Inbox related to the subject "History questions."

11. Save the messages you found as HTML files in the **Tutorial.01\Cases** folder included with your Data Files.

12. File the found messages in the Answers folder, and then close the Find bar.

13. File the message with the vCard in the Answers folder.

14. Use the Organize pane to display all the messages in the Answers folder from yourself in green.

15. Archive the Answers subfolder as **Answers Archive** in the **Tutorial.01\Cases** folder included with your Data Files. Close the archive.

16. Delete the Answers folder, the messages in the Sent Items folder, and the contact, and then empty the Deleted Items folder.

Challenge

Extend what you've learned to create e-mail invitations for a graduation party.

Case Problem 2

There are no Data Files needed for this Case Problem.

Party Planners Jace Moran, owner of Party Planners, plans events ranging from company picnics to children's birthday parties to weddings. Right now, she is working on a graduation party. The graduate hosting the party has given Jace the e-mail addresses for the entire guest list so that Jace can send the invitations using Outlook. Complete the following:

Explore

1. Create a new e-mail message to your e-mail address with an appropriate subject using an Excel worksheet as the message body. With the Inbox selected, click Actions on the menu bar, point to New Mail Message Using, point to Microsoft Office, and then click Microsoft Excel Worksheet. In column A, enter a list of foods for the party. In column B, enter the probable cost for the food. Total the cost column. Send the e-mail to the Outbox and then to your mail server. Close Excel without saving the worksheet.

2. Create contact cards for five guests. Include their names, addresses, phone numbers, and e-mail addresses. Enter your own e-mail address for each contact. Create a contact card for Jace Moran that includes her name, company name, and your e-mail address.

3. Create a distribution list named "Guests" that includes the contact cards of all the guests.

4. Edit three contacts to include one item of personal information, such as a birthday or spouse's name.

Explore

5. Use stationery to create the party invitation. From the Inbox, click Actions on the menu bar, point to New Mail Message Using, and then click More Stationery. Click an appropriate stationery in the Stationery list box, and then click the OK button.

Explore

6. Address the invitation to the Guests distribution list and to Jace. Type an appropriate subject.

7. Enter the Day, Time, and Place of the party. Format the stationery using Word's formatting features; try changing the font and color of existing text. Send the message to the Outbox and then to your mail server.

8. Create a Mail and Post Items subfolder named "Party" in the Inbox, and then move the food cost e-mail into the Party subfolder.

9. Read and print the food cost e-mail, and then add a purple flag to the message.

10. Create a rule that moves any messages with the subject you used for the invitation into the Party subfolder.

11. Switch to the Contacts folder, and then change the view to Detailed Address Cards.

Explore

12. Print the contact cards you created. If other contact cards exist in addition to the ones you created, press and hold the Ctrl key as you click the contact name for each card you created. Open the Print dialog box. Use Card Style as the Print style and, if you selected contact cards, click the Only selected items option button in the Print range. Click the OK button.

Explore

13. Create a Contacts subfolder named "Guests" located in the Contacts folder and move the contact cards you created into it. (*Hint*: Make sure you change the Folder contains list box to "Contact Items" in the Create New Folder dialog box.)

Explore

14. Export your contact list. Click File on the menu bar, and then click Import and Export. Click Export to a file, and then click the Next button. Click Microsoft Access, and then click the Next button. If necessary, click the plus button next to Contacts to display the Guests subfolder, select the subfolder, and then click the Next button. Use the Browse button to save the file as **Guest List** to the **Tutorial.01\Cases** folder included with your Data Files. Click the Next button, and then click the Finish button. The contact list is exported as an Access database.

15. Download your messages. (Note that you will only receive one message because all of the e-mail addresses for your contacts are the same.) Print the message, and then save it as an HTML file to the **Tutorial.01\Cases** folder included with your Data Files.

16. Archive the messages in the Party subfolder as **Party Archive** in the **Tutorial.01\Cases** folder included with your Data Files.

Explore

17. Expand the Archive folder files, and then copy the Guests subfolder to the archive. Click the Guests subfolder, press and hold the Ctrl key as you drag the folder to the archive file, and then release the Ctrl key. Close the archive file.

18. Delete the rule you created, the Guests subfolder, the Party subfolder, the messages in the Sent Items folder, and the contacts you created, and then empty the Deleted Items folder.

Review

Quick Check Answers

Session 1.1

1. The Inbox stores e-mail messages you have received; the Outbox stores e-mail messages you have written but not yet sent.

2. The electronic transfer of messages between computers on the Internet. It's an inexpensive way to communicate with others who are nearby or far away. You can send and read messages at your convenience.

3. Text that is automatically added to every e-mail message you send, such as your name, job title, and company name.

4. a contact's name, job title, company name and address, phone and fax numbers, as well as personal information such as birthdays, anniversaries, and children's names

5. Creates a contact card for a group of people to whom you frequently send the same messages; a distribution list saves time and insures that you don't inadvertently leave out someone.

Session 1.2

1. Reply responds to only the sender of the e-mail message; Reply to All responds to the sender and any other recipients of the e-mail message.

2. False

3. Drag the message from the Inbox pane to the subfolder in the Folder List.

4. folders that display any e-mail messages that match specific search criteria; messages are stored in their current Outlook folder.

5. specifies how Outlook should process and organize your e-mail messages.

6. moves items you selected from Outlook into a personal folder file

Objectives

Session 2.1
- Write notes
- Customize views with fields
- Create and assign tasks
- Respond to an assigned task
- Organize tasks by categories
- Schedule appointments and events in the Calendar

Session 2.2
- Plan a meeting
- Respond to a meeting request
- Save a calendar as a Web page
- Filter and sort contacts
- Perform a mail merge in Word from Outlook
- Record activities in the Journal
- Communicate with instant messages

Integrating Outlook Components and Office

Planning a Meeting

Case

The Express Lane

Alan Gregory and Lora Shaw are planning to expand The Express Lane's Web site. They have hired Lucinda Tores, a Web site design specialist, to redesign the look of the site, update and maintain its content, and expand the information presented. Currently, the Web site contains information about The Express Lane—its purpose, history, goals, and, of course, its available products. Lucinda has some ideas for expanding the content, by adding things such as health and natural foods features, supplier spotlights, and food tips. Using Outlook, she can jot down notes about the Web site, plan her schedule, organize meetings regarding the Web site, and even write form letters to all suppliers asking for their input.

Although each of the six Outlook components functions independently, all of them can be integrated smoothly. You have already seen how you can address e-mail messages using a contact list. In addition, you can move any item from one folder to another to create another item. In this tutorial, you'll write notes and add them to your task list. You'll assign a task to someone else, using e-mail to send the request. You'll schedule an appointment in the Calendar to block out time to complete the task. You'll plan a meeting and send e-mail invitations to attendees. You'll create a Journal entry from a contact to record an activity. Finally, you'll use instant messaging to send messages.

You can also integrate Outlook smoothly with other Office programs. You can create and use many Office documents directly from Outlook. For example, you can save the Calendar as an HTML document to post on an intranet or the Internet. You can import a contact list from Access, Excel, or Word. You can create letters to one or more contacts, using the letter-writing features in Word. Although you won't try it in this tutorial, you can also create an e-mail message using a Word document, PowerPoint slide, Excel worksheet, or Access data access page for the body text.

Student Data Files

▼**Tutorial.02**

▽ **Tutorial folder**
   Contacts.mdb
   Letter.doc

▽ **Review folder**
   Contacts.xls

▽ **Cases folder**
   Answers.mdb
   Guest List.mdb

Jotting Down Notes

Outlook comes with an electronic notepad, called Notes. You can use Notes to jot down and organize your ideas, questions, and reminders. You can leave a note open on the screen as you work or you can close it, knowing that it will never get buried under a file or inadvertently tossed in the garbage.

Remember, you can use the New button's list arrow to select any new Outlook item, regardless of which folder is displayed. This way, you can create a note when the idea hits, no matter which folder you are working with at the time. Before you create a note, you'll use the New button to create a contact card for yourself without changing folders.

To create a contact card:

1. Click the **Mail** button in the Navigation Pane, if necessary, click the **New** button list arrow on the Standard toolbar, and then click **Contact**. A new Contact window opens.

2. Enter contact information for yourself, including your name and e-mail address.

3. Save and close the contact card.

   Trouble? If the Duplicate Contact Detected dialog box opens, you already have a contact with the same name or e-mail address. Click the Add this as a new contact anyway option button, and then click the OK button.

You'll create several notes to remind you of the items for your calendar.

To create a note:

1. Click the **New** button list arrow on the Standard toolbar, and then click **Note**. A square, yellow note appears, labeled with the date and time.

   Trouble? If your note is not yellow or does not show the date and time, then your Notes settings have been changed. Click the Close button ☒ in the upper-right corner of the note to close it. Click Tools on the menu bar, click Options, click the Preferences tab, if necessary, and then click the Note Options button. If necessary, change the color to Yellow and the size to Medium, and then click the OK button. Click the Other tab in the Options dialog box, click the Advanced Options button, click the When viewing Notes, show time and date check box to insert a check mark, and then click the OK button in each dialog box. Repeat Step 1.

2. Type **Web site ideas: food storage and preparation tips; health studies; seasonal recipes** as the note text. See Figure 2-1.

Figure 2-1 ▶ **Outlook note**

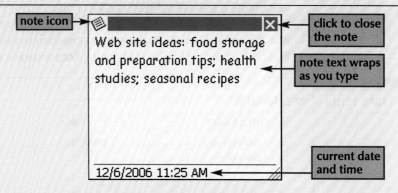

- note icon
- click to close the note
- note text wraps as you type
- current date and time

Web site ideas: food storage and preparation tips; health studies; seasonal recipes

12/6/2006 11:25 AM

You can associate a note, or any Outlook item, with a contact. This enables you to find all items linked to specific contact, no matter what folder they are stored in. You'll add yourself as the contact for this note.

▶ **3.** Click the **Notes** icon 📝 in the upper-left corner of the open note, and then click **Contacts**. The Contacts for Note dialog box opens.

▶ **4.** Click the **Contacts** button to open the Select Contacts dialog box, make sure Contacts is selected in the Look in list at the top of the dialog box, click your name in the Items list, and then click the **OK** button. Your name appears in the text box in the Contacts for Note dialog box.

▶ **5.** Click the **Close** button in the Contacts for Note dialog box. You are assigned as a contact for the note.

Notes remain open until you close them, and can float on top of any open Office program.

▶ **6.** Click the **Close** button ❎ in the upper-right corner of the note to close it.

▶ **7.** Create a second note with the text **More Web site ideas: supplier spotlights and natural cleaning methods**, assign yourself as the contact, and then close the note.

▶ **8.** Create a third note with the text **Plan meeting about Web site ideas**, don't assign a contact, and then close that note.

To display a closed note, you can double-click it in the Notes folder. You can edit the text in an open note, just as you can edit the text in any document.

Organizing Notes

There are several ways to organize notes. You can customize your notes with different colors to help organize them. You decide to leave informational notes as yellow and change task notes to blue.

To change the note color:

▶ **1.** Click the **Notes** button 📝 in the Navigation Pane to switch to the Notes folder.

▶ **2.** Right-click the **Plan meeting** note, and then point to **Color** on the shortcut menu. You can select from a variety of colors.

▶ **3.** Click **Blue**. The note changes to blue.

▶ **4.** Click outside the note to deselect it. See Figure 2-2.

Figure 2-2	Notes folder

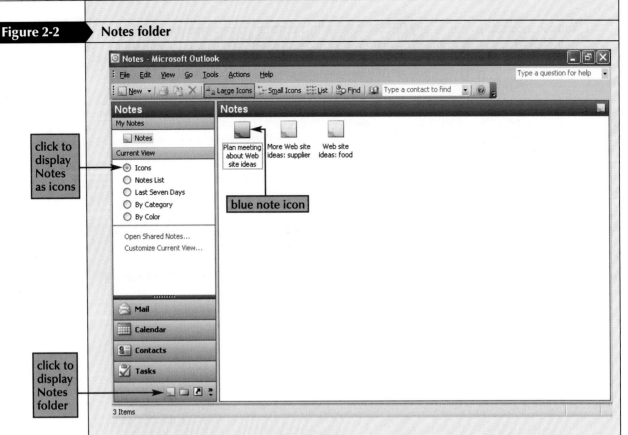

Trouble? If your notes are not displayed as icons, click the Icons option button in the Current View pane in the Navigation pane.

Another way to organize your notes is to assign each note to a category. A **category** is a keyword or phrase that you assign to an item to help organize and later locate related items, regardless of whether they are stored in the same folder. For example, you might create a Web Site category and assign it to any notes, tasks, contacts, e-mail messages, and meetings related to creating and maintaining the company Web site. You can assign items to general categories from the Master Category List, such as Business and Personal, or to more specific categories that you add to the master list, such as Web Site and Warehouse. You can also assign items to more than one category; for example, you could assign a site to Web Site and Phone Calls.

Reference Window | **Creating and Assigning Categories**

- Click the Categories button at the bottom of the item window.
- Click the Master Category List button.
- Type a category name in the New category text box, and then click the Add button.
- Click the OK button.
- Click the categories you want to assign to the item, and then click the OK button.
- Save and close the item.

You'll add a category called "Web Site" and assign the three notes to it.

To assign notes to categories:

1. Right-click the **Web site ideas** note, and then click **Categories** on the shortcut menu. The Categories dialog box opens with a list of available categories. Because "Web Site" is not on this default list, you'll create it.

2. Click the **Master Category List** button. The Master Category List dialog box opens.

   Category names are case sensitive, which means that Outlook sees "Web Site," "web site," and "WEB SITE" as different categories.

3. Type **Web Site** in the New category text box, and then click the **Add** button to enter the category in the list.

4. Click the **OK** button to return to the Categories dialog box.

5. Scroll down and click the **Web Site** check box in the Available categories list to insert a check mark. See Figure 2-3.

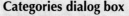

Categories dialog box | Figure 2-3

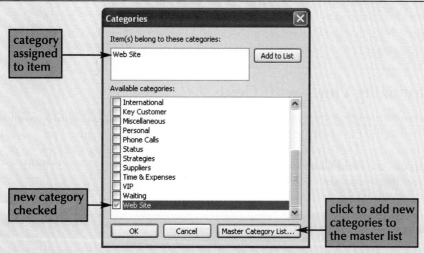

category assigned to item

new category checked

click to add new categories to the master list

6. Click the **OK** button. Like assigned contacts, the assigned category is not visible in the note.

7. Assign the **Web Site** category to the More Web site ideas and Plan meeting notes.

8. Assign the **Strategies** category to the Plan meeting note.

The three notes are assigned to the same category, and one note, the Plan meeting note, is also assigned to a second category. Once you've assigned categories to Outlook items, you can use the Advanced Find command to locate all items associated with a specific category.

From the Notes folder, you can organize the notes in a variety of views, including by color, date, and category. The Current View pane in the Navigation Pane provides a quick way to switch between the available views for the Notes folder.

To organize and view notes:

1. Click the **By Color** option button in the Current View pane in the Navigation Pane. The existing notes are grouped by color—in this case, blue and yellow. See Figure 2-4.

Figure 2-4 **Notes folder in By Color view**

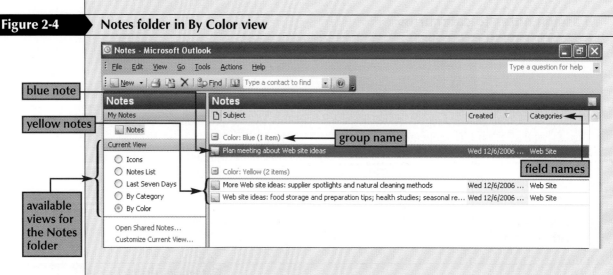

2. Click the **By Category** option button in the Current View pane in the Navigation Pane. The notes are grouped by category—in this case, the Web Site category and the Strategies category. Note that the Plan meeting note now appears twice, once in each category.

Customizing Views with Fields

The default views that are available for each folder provide a good starting point for looking at items. But the ability to add fields to or remove fields from any view as well as to select the order in which those fields appear is part of what makes Outlook so powerful. You can use the **Field Chooser**, a window that contains a list of available fields you can add to an item or a view, to show exactly the fields you want.

Reference Window | **Customizing Views with Fields**

- Switch to the view you want to customize.
- To add a field to the current view, right-click the column headers, click Field Chooser, drag a field from the Field Chooser to the appropriate location within the column headings, using the red arrows to position the field, and then click the Close button in the Field Chooser title bar.
- To reorder column headings, drag a column heading to a new location within the column headings, using the red arrows to position the field.
- To remove a field from the current view, drag the field from the column headings into the main folder.

Two of the notes you created include the Contact field, but this field does not appear in any of the standard Notes views. You'll use the Field Chooser to customize the By Category view to display this field.

To add a field to a view:

1. Right-click the gray column headings banner in the Notes folder, and then click **Field Chooser** on the shortcut menu. The Field Chooser opens, displaying the Frequently-used fields list.

   Trouble? If the Field Chooser command does not appear on the shortcut menu, your Outlook window is probably not maximized. Click a blank area of the screen to close the shortcut menu, click the maximize button ☐ in the Outlook window title bar, and then repeat Step 1.

2. Click the list arrow next to **Frequently-used fields**, and then click **All Note fields**. All the Notes fields not currently in the displayed view are listed.

3. Drag the **Contacts** field from the Field Chooser to the right of the Created field, using the red placement arrows that appear to position the field. The field is added to the view as the fourth column.

4. Click the **Close** button ☒ on the Field Chooser title bar.

You can reorder fields in a view to display the information in a more logical organization. For example, the Contacts field is more important in this case than the Created field so you can reposition the field by dragging it by its column heading to a new location. You can also quickly remove unwanted fields from a table view, such as the By Color view, by dragging the fields off the table by their column headings.

To reposition and remove a field from a view:

1. Drag the **Contacts** field to between the Subject and Created fields, using the red placement arrows to position the field. The field is moved to become the third column.

2. Drag the **Contacts** field by its column heading off of the gray bar until a big X appears over the field, and then release the mouse button. The field is removed from the view.

3. Click the **Icons** option button in the Current View pane in the Navigation Pane. The notes are displayed as icons.

Creating a Task List

A **task** is any action you need to complete and want to track, similar to items on a to-do list. A task can occur once, such as planning a meeting, or repeatedly (called a **recurring task**), such as sending a monthly status report. A task can simply list something you need to complete, or it can include more details, such as a due date, start date, status, priority, percentage complete, and other notes. When you finish a task, you can mark it complete.

You can create a task from scratch or from an existing Outlook item. The **AutoCreate** feature generates a new item when you drag an item from one folder to another. For example, dragging a note into the Tasks folder creates a task, and dragging an e-mail message into the Calendar folder creates an appointment. Outlook inserts relevant information from the original item into the appropriate fields in the new item and places the contents of the original item in the text box.

You'll use AutoCreate to set up a task by moving the blue note from the Notes folder to the Tasks folder.

To create a task from a note:

1. Drag the **blue note** to the **Tasks** button in the Navigation Pane. A Task window titled Plan meeting about Web site ideas with information from the note opens. The text of the note appears in the Subject text box, and the complete note text, the date the note was modified, and the categories assigned to the note (and now the task), appear in the text pane at the bottom of the Task window.

2. Click the **Due date** list arrow, and then click tomorrow's date to assign a deadline for the task.

3. Click the **Priority** list arrow, and then click **High** to change the task's urgency level. See Figure 2-5.

Figure 2-5 | Task window

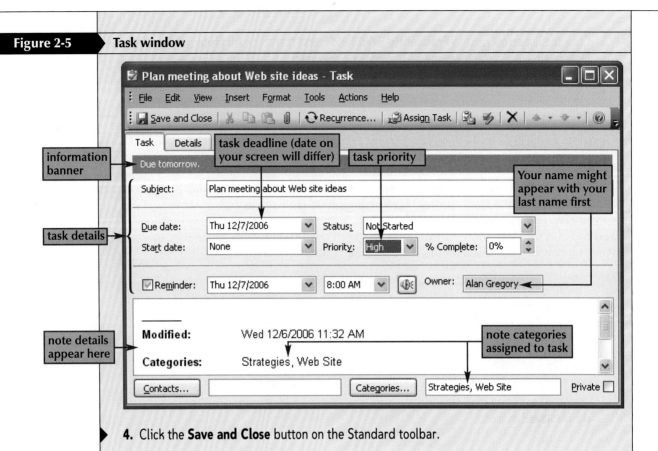

4. Click the **Save and Close** button on the Standard toolbar.

Next, you'll switch to the Tasks folder to view the new task and create additional tasks.

To create a one-time task from the Tasks folder:

1. Click the **Tasks** button in the Navigation Pane. The Tasks folder appears. You want to use the view that displays a list of task subjects and due dates.

2. If necessary, click the **Simple List** option button in the Current View pane in the Navigation Pane. The tasks appear in a list, and a placeholder text box at the top of the list indicates that you can click it to add a new task. See Figure 2-6.

Figure 2-6 | Tasks folder

3. Click the **Click here to add a new Task** text box, and then type **Contact suppliers for spotlight features** as the subject of the task.

4. Press the **Tab** key to move to the Due Date text box, type **next Tuesday**, and then press the **Enter** key to save the task. Outlook converts the text description of the due date to the correct calendar date and adds the task to the top of the Task list.

The **AutoDate** feature converts natural-language date and time descriptions, such as one week from today and noon, into the numerical format that represents the month, day, and year or time, respectively. You can also type abbreviations, such as Wed or Feb, and holiday names with or without punctuation, such as New Year's Day. To remove a date or time, just type "none" in the text box. You could also click in the Due Date text box, click the list arrow that appears to display a calendar, and then click a date.

The Simple List view shows only a few fields of information; other views, however, display more fields. To enter other information, you might change the view. For example, in Detailed List view, which also shows each task's status, percentage complete, and assigned categories, you could click the Status text box for the "Contact suppliers" task and select "Waiting on someone else." You could also open the Task window for any task by double-clicking its name in the task list and then entering the necessary data.

Assigning Tasks to Others

You own the tasks you created, which means that you are responsible for completing them. Sometimes, however, you'll want to assign tasks to someone else. For example, Alan Gregory wants to assign the task to update the look of the company Web site to Lucinda Tores, the Web site design specialist. Each assigned task involves two people—one to send a **task request** (an e-mail message with details about the task to be assigned) and one to respond to the task request. The person who sends the task request transfers ownership of the task to the other person, although the original owner can keep an updated copy of the task in the task list and receive status reports. You cannot assign a task to yourself because you initially own any task you create. The person to whom you assign a task must be using Outlook to send and receive e-mail.

Assigning a Task

Reference Window

- Click the New Task button on the Standard toolbar.
- Click the Assign Task button on the Standard toolbar.
- Enter recipient's e-mail address in the To text box.
- Click the Send button on the Standard toolbar.
- Click the OK button in the confirmation dialog box.

To complete the steps in this section and the Responding to a Task Request section, you'll need to work with a classmate who is also using Outlook 2003 to send and receive e-mail. If you don't have a classmate to work with, ask your instructor for an e-mail address you can use. Otherwise, you should read but not complete these sections.

To assign a task to another person:

1. Click the **New** button on the Standard toolbar. A new Task window opens.

2. Create a task using the subject **Web site design update** with a due date **two months from today** and a **High** priority. Leave the task open.

3. Click the **Assign Task** button on the Standard toolbar in the Task window. The Task window changes to include a To text box for specifying the task recipient. See Figure 2-7.

Figure 2-7 **Task window for assignment**

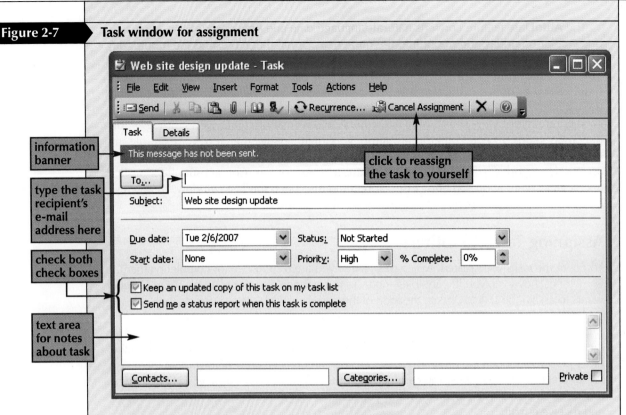

Notice the two new check boxes. The Keep an updated copy of this task on my task list check box creates a copy of the task in your task list. You then receive updates when the assigned owner changes the task. The Send me a status report when this task is complete check box specifies that you receive a message that the task is complete when the new owner finishes it.

4. Type a classmate's e-mail address in the To text box. You could also address the task to anyone in the Contacts folder, just as you would address an e-mail message.

   Trouble? If you don't have a classmate's e-mail address, you can read but not complete the rest of the steps in this section or those in the section "Responding to a Task Request."

5. Click the **Send** button on the Standard toolbar.

6. Click the **OK** button to confirm that the task reminder for this message is turned off. The task icon in the Tasks list changes to ▒ to indicate that it has been assigned.

7. Send the message to your mail server, if necessary.

While waiting for the task request to arrive, you decide to organize your tasks.

Organizing Tasks with Categories

Like notes, you can assign tasks to categories.

To assign tasks to a category:

1. In the Tasks folder, double-click the **Contact suppliers for spotlight features** task to open its Task window.

2. Click the **Categories** button at the bottom of the Task window. The Categories dialog box opens.

3. Click the **Web Site** check box in the Available categories list, and then click the **OK** button. The Categories text box shows the selected category.

4. Click the **Save and Close** button on the Standard toolbar to close the task.

5. Double-click the **Plan meeting about Web site ideas** task to open it, verify that the **Strategies** and **Web Site** categories are assigned, and then save and close the task.

The Simple List view shows whether the tasks are assigned, whether they are complete, and when they are due, but no information appears about their categories, status, or priority. To see these specifics, you'll change the view.

To view tasks by categories:

1. Click the **By Category** option button in the Current View pane in the Navigation Pane. Each group lists the tasks included in the specified category. See Figure 2-8.

Tasks grouped by category | **Figure 2-8**

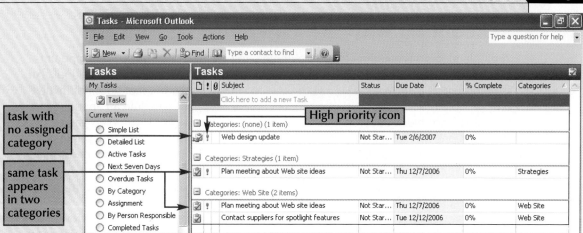

2. Click the **Simple List** option button in the Current View pane in the Navigation Pane.

Responding to a Task Request

The person who receives a task request becomes the new owner of the task and can accept, decline, or reassign that task. By accepting the task, the recipient becomes the permanent owner and the only person who can update the task. If the recipient declines the task, it returns to the original owner. Recipients who assign the task to someone else can no longer change the task, but they can keep it in their task list and receive status reports, just like the original owner. Only the current task owner can update a task. If the task was assigned to other people before the current task owner, every change the owner makes to the task is copied automatically to the task in the previous owners' task lists. When the current owner completes the task, the previous owners receive a status report.

To respond to a task request:

1. Switch to the Inbox, and then click the **Send/Receive** button on the Standard toolbar to receive the task request e-mail in your Inbox if it is not already there, and then click the

e-mail message to select it, if necessary. The name of the person who assigned the task and the date on which it was assigned appears in the message in the Reading Pane.

Trouble? If the message does not appear, wait a few minutes and then try again. If it still does not appear, verify that your classmate has sent the task request to you.

▶ 2. Click the **Accept** button in the Reading Pane to accept the request. If you wanted to reject the request, you would click the Decline button.

▶ 3. Click the **Edit the response before sending** option button, click the **OK** button, and then type **I'd be happy to complete this task.** in the text box.

▶ 4. Click the **Send** button on the Standard toolbar to move the reply to the Outbox, and then send the message to your server, if necessary.

▶ 5. Click the **Send/Receive** button on the Standard toolbar to receive the task response e-mail from your classmate in your Inbox.

To ensure that you complete all your tasks in a timely manner, you can schedule time to work on them in your calendar.

Scheduling with the Calendar

The Calendar is a scheduling tool for planning and recording your upcoming appointments, events, and meetings. Each of these terms has a special meaning in Outlook. An **appointment** is an activity that you schedule in your calendar but that does not involve other people or resources. For example, Lucinda Tores might schedule an appointment in her calendar to block out time for the task of redesigning the company Web page. An **event** is a one-time or annual activity that lasts 24 hours or more, such as a seminar, trade show, or vacation. A **meeting** is an appointment to which you invite people or for which you reserve resources, including conference rooms and projection equipment. Meetings can take place either face-to-face or online. Just as with tasks, you can send and receive meeting requests only if you use Outlook to send and receive e-mail.

The Day, Week, and Month views are the most commonly used Calendar views. They resemble traditional planner books, providing space for recording events, appointments, and meetings. Table views show lists of active appointments, recurring meetings, events, and so on. Calendar views are available on the View menu.

To navigate within the Calendar:

▶ 1. Click the **Calendar** button in the Navigation Pane. In Day/Week/Month view, the Calendar Standard toolbar contains buttons that change the way you view the planner—as a daily, weekly, or monthly calendar.

▶ 2. Click **View** on the menu bar, point to **Arrange By**, point to **Current View**, and then click **Day/Week/Month**, if necessary. Buttons on the Standard toolbar enable you to switch between each of these views.

▶ 3. Click the **Day** button on the Standard toolbar to display the calendar as a daily planner. See Figure 2-9.

Calendar in Day view ◄ **Figure 2-9**

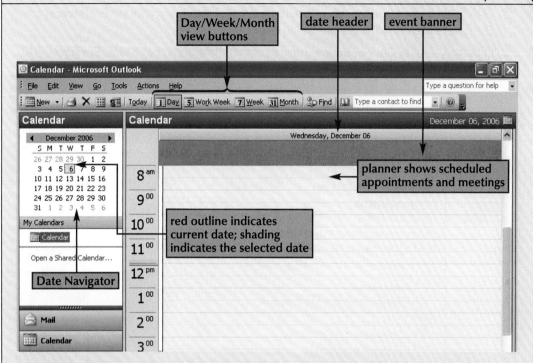

4. Click the **Week** button on the Standard toolbar to display the calendar as a seven-day planner.

5. Click the **Month** button on the Standard toolbar to display the calendar as a one-month planner.

6. Click the **Day** button on the Standard toolbar to return to Day view.

7. Click the date for next Monday on the Date Navigator. That date becomes shaded in the Date Navigator, and the planner changes to show that day's schedule.

8. Click the scroll arrow on the right of the Date Navigator title bar to move to the next month's calendar. You can quickly display any month or date.

9. Click the **Today** button on the Standard toolbar. The calendar returns to the current day's planner.

Changing the Calendar view enables you to display your schedule in a variety of formats, depending on your current needs.

Configuring Calendar Options

Outlook is quite functional with its default settings. However, it also has many optional settings. At some point, you may want to fine-tune some of these settings to better fit the way you work. There are options available for each Outlook folder and function.

The Options dialog box provides access to most of the customization options for Outlook. They are organized by categories and subcategories within the tabs. You'll open the Options dialog box and change some of the Calendar options.

You'll start by modifying the times Outlook displays as the workday, or usual business hours. Because of its morning and evening deliveries, The Express Lane office opens at 7 a.m. and closes at 8 p.m.—two hours earlier and three hours later than usual business hours. It's also open on Saturdays. You can change the Calendar options to reflect this shifted work day and work week.

To configure Calendar options:

1. Click **Tools** on the menu bar, click **Options**, and then, if necessary, click the **Preferences** tab. The Preferences tab in the Options dialog box opens.

2. Click the **Calendar Options** button. The Calendar Options dialog box opens. See Figure 2-10.

Figure 2-10 Calendar Options dialog box

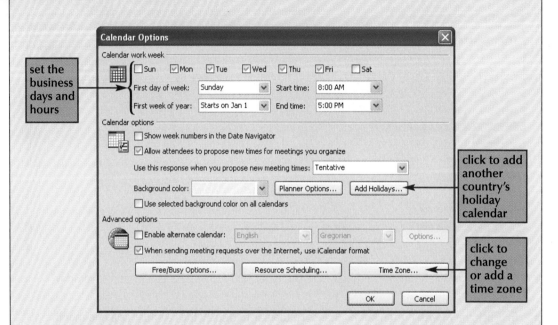

You can change the days considered part of the workweek, specify the standard hours counted as the workday, and set which days at the start of the year are counted as workdays. You can also add another country's holidays to the Calendar.

3. Click the **Sat** check box to insert a check mark.

4. Click the **Start time** list arrow, and then click **7:00 AM**.

5. Click the **End time** list arrow, and then click **8:00 PM**.

6. Click the **OK** button in the Calendar Options dialog box, and then click the **OK** button in the Options dialog box.

7. Scroll up the planner to display 5 a.m. The light yellow, indicating the workday hours, has shifted to reflect your changes. See Figure 2-11.

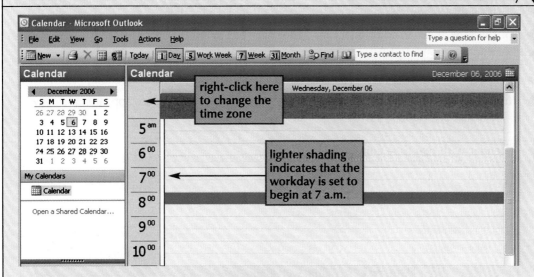

Trouble? If you don't see the change in the planner, then you might be looking at Sunday. Click another day in the Date Navigator.

In addition to these daily settings, there are some settings you can change based on your location. If you regularly work with others in another time zone, you can set up Outlook to display both zones. In addition, if you travel, you can then swap the time zones so your calendar and messages are converted to the time zone you're currently visiting.

Allen will be visiting Athens for the next six weeks. In case you need to contact him, you'll add the Athens time zone to the Calendar so that you can quickly see what time it is in Athens. Rather than reopening the Options dialog box, you can go directly to the Time Zone dialog box using a shortcut menu.

To change the time zone settings:

1. Right-click the space just above the times in the daily planner and just below the word "Calendar" (as indicated in Figure 2-11), and then click **Change Time Zone** on the shortcut menu. The Time Zone dialog box opens. See Figure 2-12.

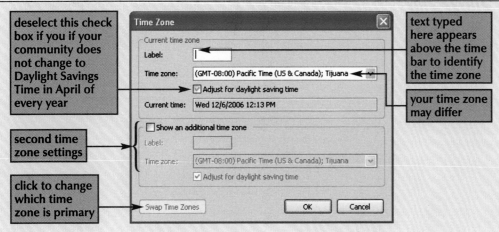

2. Type **Here** in the Label text box. This identifies your current time zone. Your time zone, daylight savings time, and current time are set for your location.

3. Click the **Show an additional time zone** check box to insert a check mark.

4. Type **Athens** in the Label text box. This identifies Allen's time zone.

5. Click the **Time zone** list arrow, and then click **(GMT+02:00) Athens, Istanbul, Minsk**.

6. Click the **OK** button in the Time Zone dialog box. The two time zones appear in the daily planner. See Figure 2-13.

Figure 2-13 ▶ **Calendar with two time zone**

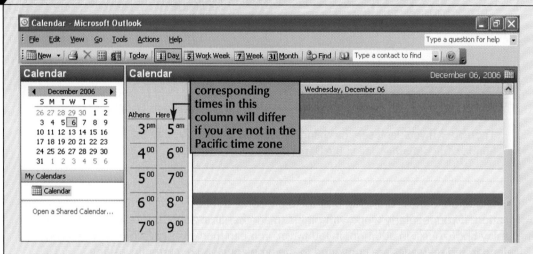

Trouble? If the times listed in the Here time bar differ from those shown in Figure 2-13, you are located in a different time zone than Pacific Standard Time.

One final customization you want to make to the Calendar is to display the **TaskPad**, which is a list of tasks in the Tasks folder that you can display in the Calendar.

To display the TaskPad in the Calendar:

1. Click **View** on the menu bar, and then click **TaskPad**. The Date Navigator shifts to the right of the planner and the TaskPad is displayed below the Date Navigator. See Figure 2-14.

   Trouble? If the TaskPad is not visible on your screen, then it probably was open already. Repeat Step 1.

Calendar with TaskPad ◄ Figure 2-14

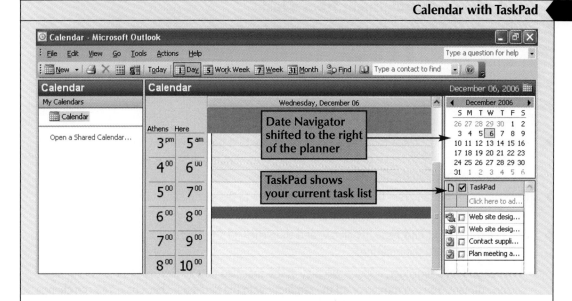

There are many other options you can use to customize Outlook to match your personal work style and preferences.

Scheduling Appointments

You can schedule and change appointments in your own calendar, and you can give others (who use Outlook) permission to do the same. Likewise, other people can give you permission to make and modify schedules in their calendars. To let people know about your availability, you can specify how time is blocked out for an appointment, as indicated in Figure 2-15. Other people cannot see an appointment marked as private, even if they have permission to access your calendar.

Appointment availability codes ◄ Figure 2-15

Time Shown As	Border Color	Availability to Others
Busy	solid blue	unavailable
Free	clear	available
Tentative	blue and white stripes	available
Out of office	solid purple	unavailable

You can then color-code each appointment, meeting, or event, using the Calendar Coloring button on the Standard toolbar. Each color denotes a different purpose, such as red for important, blue for business, green for personal, and so forth. So an important, tentative appointment would appear in your calendar as red with a blue striped border, and an important, busy appointment would appear as red with a solid blue border.

Although you can create an appointment using the New Appointment button on the Standard toolbar, you can also schedule an appointment by dragging a task from the Tasks folder or the Calendar TaskPad to the planner. You'll use the latter method to schedule an appointment for completing the Plan meeting about Web site ideas task.

To schedule an appointment from a task:

1. Drag the **Plan meeting about Web site ideas** task from the TaskPad onto the planner. An Appointment window opens. The task's subject and categories are already assigned to the appointment. You could edit the subject or assign additional categories if needed.

2. If necessary, maximize the window.

3. Type **Lucinda's Office** in the Location text box to record the place where the appointment will occur.

4. Press the **Tab** key twice to move to the **Start time** text box, type **next Tuesday**, and then press the **Tab** key to move to the second Start time text box. The correct date for next Tuesday appears in the first Start time text box.

5. Type **ten**, and then press the **Tab** key twice to move to the second End time text box. The end time is already set to next Tuesday's date because the end time cannot precede the start time.

6. Click the second **End time** list arrow, and then click **11:00 AM (1 hour)** to enter the time you need to plan the meeting.

   When you set a reminder, a sound will play at the specified time to alert you to the upcoming appointment. You can turn on or off the reminder with the Reminder check box. You can change the reminder time by selecting a time from the list or typing a new time in the text box.

7. If necessary, click the **Reminder** check box to insert a check mark, click the **Reminder** list arrow, and then click **5 minutes**.

8. Click the **Show time as** list arrow, and then click **Tentative**. Thus, if anything urgent comes up, this block of time appears as available on your calendar.

9. Click the **Label** list arrow, and then click **Needs Preparation**. See Figure 2-16.

Figure 2-16	Completed Appointment window

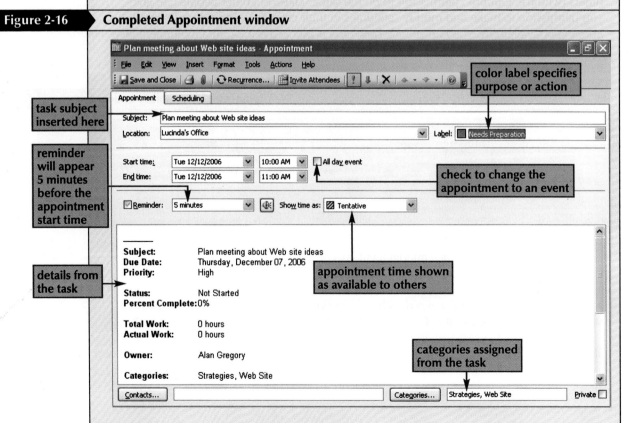

10. Click the **Save and Close** button on the Standard toolbar. The appointment is added to your calendar.

Next Tuesday's date appears in boldface in the Date Navigator, indicating that you have an appointment scheduled on that day. You also can schedule appointments by selecting the date and time in the planner and then typing the appointment subject. You'll schedule a second appointment for next Tuesday.

To schedule a second appointment:

▶ 1. Click next Tuesday's date in the Date Navigator, and then scroll up the planner until **8:00 a.m** in your time zone is the top time block in the planner. You see the appointment you just scheduled in the 10:00 to 11:00 a.m. time block, with the indicator bar on the left colored to indicate that this appointment is tentative.

▶ 2. Click **2:00** in your time zone to select the 2:00 to 2:30 block, and then drag to select the next three half-hour blocks as well. The 2:00 to 4:00 block of time changes to blue to indicate that it's selected.

▶ 3. Type **Create meeting agenda**, and then press the **Enter** key. The solid blue border indicates that the appointment is shown as Busy in your calendar.

▶ 4. Click the **Calendar Coloring** button ▦ on the Standard toolbar, and then click **Important** to color-code the appointment. See Figure 2-17.

Calendar with appointments 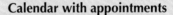 **Figure 2-17**

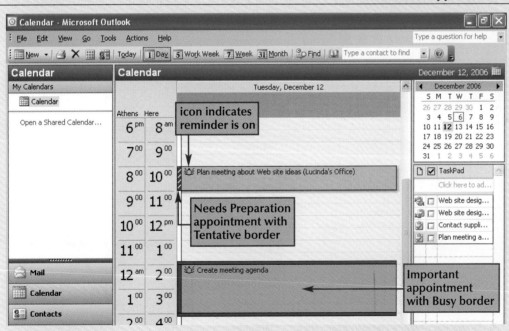

After looking at both appointments, you decide to create the meeting agenda before you plan the meeting, and you decide that you will need only one hour to do this.

▶ 5. Position the pointer over the bottom edge of the second appointment so that it changes to ↕, and then drag the border up so that the appointment block is only one hour (from 2:00 p.m. to 3:00 p.m.).

▶ 6. Position the pointer over the left border of the appointment so that it changes to ✛, and then drag the entire appointment up so that it occurs from **9:00 a.m.** to **10:00 a.m.**.

The Web site team will meet every week for the next month, and you will need to create an agenda for each meeting. Rather than schedule the same appointment for each of the next three weeks, you decide to make this appointment recurring. A **recurring appointment** repeats on a regular basis, such as weekly or on the third Tuesday of the month. To schedule a new recurring appointment, you can click the Actions menu, click New Recurring Appointment, and then enter the recurrence information along with the appointment information. Also, you can change an existing appointment to a recurring appointment.

Reference Window	**Scheduling a Recurring Appointment**

- Open or create an appointment.
- Click the Recurrence button on the Standard toolbar.
- Set recurrence pattern and range.
- Click the OK button.
- Save and close the appointment.

To schedule a recurring appointment:

1. Double-click the **Create meeting agenda** appointment to open its Appointment window.

2. Click the **Recurrence** button on the Standard toolbar. The Appointment Recurrence dialog box opens. See Figure 2-18.

Figure 2-18	Appointment Recurrence dialog box

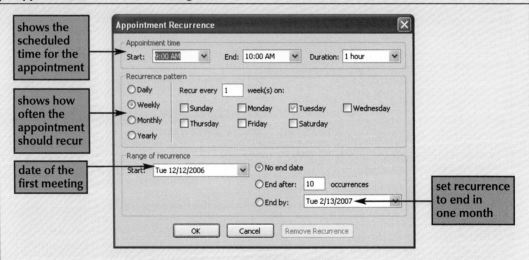

3. In the Recurrence pattern area, click the **Weekly** option button, if necessary, and make sure that this appointment is set to Recur every **1** week(s) on **Tuesday**.

4. In the Range of recurrence section make sure that the Start list box shows next Tuesday's date, click the **End by** option button, and then type **one month** in the End by text box.

5. Click the **OK** button. While you have the appointment open, you'll assign categories.

6. Use the **Categories** button to add the **Strategies** and **Web Site** categories to the appointment.

7. Click the **Save and Close** button on the Standard toolbar.

Time is now blocked out each Tuesday for the next month to plan the meeting agenda, as indicated by the bold dates in the Date Navigator. Also, the recurrence icon ⟳ appears below the reminder bell 🔔 in the appointment.

Scheduling Events

Events are blocks of time that last from midnight to midnight. They can occur for one or more days, such as a one-day training seminar or a three-day health fair. Unlike appointments, events are always scheduled as free time in your calendar. This is so you can schedule appointments during an event; for example, at an all-day seminar, you can schedule an appointment with a colleague to discuss a presentation.

You schedule a one-day event and a multiday event in similar fashion. In Day/Week/Month view, you can quickly create an event by double-clicking the date heading of the day of the event.

To schedule an event:

1. Click the **Work Week** button on the Standard toolbar to display the six workdays for next week in the Calendar.

2. Click the date heading for next **Wednesday**. The box below the date changes to white, indicating that you can type in it. This action would create a one-day event. Instead, you want to create a two-day event.

3. Drag to select the date headings for **Wednesday** and **Thursday**. Both boxes are white.

4. Type **Training Seminar** as the event subject, and then press the **Enter** key.

   You want to change the reminder option and add a location for the event.

5. Double-click the event heading **Training Seminar**. The Training Seminar Event window opens. Because the All day event check box is selected, the window provides fewer options.

   Trouble? If a new Event window opens, you probably clicked the date heading rather than the event heading. Close the Event window, position the pointer on the event heading, and then double-click.

   Trouble? If a new text box opens below the Training Seminar event in the date heading, press the Esc key, and then repeat Step 5.

6. In the Location text box, type **Conference Room**.

7. Click the **Reminder** check box to remove the check mark and turn off the reminder.

8. Click the **Save and Close** button on the Standard toolbar. See Figure 2-19.

Calendar with an event | **Figure 2-19**

Printing a Calendar

A printed calendar is helpful when you need to leave your office and want to take your schedule along. The print style options for the Calendar vary, depending on the view. In any of the Day/Week/Month views, you can select from a variety of planner-type styles. In other views, you can print selected items (called memo style) or a list of all the items (called table style) as shown in the view. Outlook changes the print specifications to match the current Calendar view. You decide to print the next work week's calendar and next Tuesday's calendar.

To print your calendar:

1. Click the **Print** button 🖳 on the Standard toolbar. The Print dialog box opens.
2. Click **Weekly Style** in the Print style area, if necessary.
3. Click the **Start** list arrow, and select next Monday's date, if necessary. It is the first day that you want to print. You can also use the AutoDate feature to set the start and end dates.
4. Type **next Friday** in the End text box, and then press the **Tab** key. Outlook changes the date to display next Friday's date, the last day that you want to print. If you wanted to print only one day, you would enter the same date in both the Start and End boxes.
5. Click the **OK** button. The calendar prints.
6. Print the calendar for **next Tuesday** in **Daily Style**.
7. Click the **Day** button on the Standard toolbar, and then click today's date in the Date Navigator on the right side of the window.

So far you have jotted down notes, created tasks, and scheduled appointments and events on your calendar. In the next session, you'll schedule the meeting for the Web site team, save your calendar as a Web page, and then use Word and Outlook to create personalized form letters. You'll also communicate with instant messages.

Review

Session 2.1 Quick Check

1. True or False? You can create a new note from any folder in Outlook.
2. Explain the difference between a task and a recurring task.
3. What happens when you drag a note to the Tasks folder?
4. What is the purpose of a category?
5. Explain the difference between an appointment, an event, and a meeting.
6. If an appointment is tentative, what color is its border?

Session 2.2

Planning a Meeting

Recall that a meeting differs from an appointment in that it includes other people and resources. When creating a meeting, you specify the people who should attend and the resources to be reserved; you also pick a date and time for the meeting. Each invitee and resource receives an e-mail message with the meeting request (they must be using Outlook as their e-mail program). You receive an e-mail reply when they respond to the request, which enables you to track who can attend and which resources are reserved. Meeting resources include conference rooms, audiovisual equipment, and other company available materials.

When you schedule a meeting, you can use the **AutoPick** feature to select the next available free time for all invitees and resources. This is generally the best way to schedule a meeting. To use AutoPick, you must have access to the shared calendars of all invitees.

Before you can reserve a resource, it must have its own mailbox on your server. The resource then becomes self-sufficient, accepting and rejecting meeting requests automatically. It accepts any invitation when it is available, and the meeting is automatically entered in the resource's calendar. The resource administrator can restrict the ability to schedule the resource. For example, if only managers are allowed to book certain conference rooms, permissions can be set so that requests from managers are accepted and requests from nonmanagers are declined.

Planning a Meeting

Reference Window

- Click Actions on the menu bar, and then click Plan a Meeting.
- Click the Add Others button, and then click Add from Address Book.
- Click a contact, and then click the Required, Optional, or Resource button.
- Click the OK button.
- AutoPick or enter meeting time, and then click the Make Meeting button.
- Type a subject and location, and then click the Send button.
- Click the Close button in the Plan a Meeting dialog box.

For The Express Lane, you'll plan a meeting with a classmate to discuss ideas for the company's Web site.

To complete the steps in this section and the Responding to a Meeting Request section, you'll need to work with a classmate who is also using Outlook 2003 to send and receive e-mail. If you don't have a classmate to work with, ask your instructor for an e-mail address to use. Otherwise, you should complete the steps in this section, but read the steps in the Responding to a Meeting Request section.

To create a contact for a classmate:

▶ 1. If you took a break after the previous session, make sure Outlook is running, the **Calendar** folder is displayed showing today's date in Day view.

▶ 2. Create a new contact for a classmate, entering the person's name and e-mail address.

Next you'll schedule a meeting with that classmate.

To schedule a meeting:

▶ 1. Click **Actions** on the menu bar, and then click **Plan a Meeting**. The Plan a Meeting dialog box opens. See Figure 2-20.

   Trouble? If the Plan a Meeting command is not on the Actions menu, you are probably in the Contacts folder. Switch back to the Calendar folder and then repeat Step 1.

Figure 2-20 **Plan a Meeting dialog box**

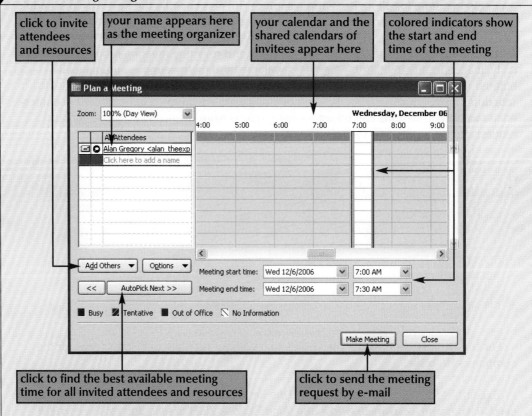

2. Click the **Add Others** button, and then click **Add from Address Book**. The Select Attendees and Resources dialog box opens.

3. Click the **Show Names from the** list arrow, and then click **Contacts**, if necessary.

4. Click your classmate's name in the contacts list, and then click the **Required** button. (The Required and Optional attendees will appear in the To text box on the Appointment tab in the Meeting window, and Resources appear in the Location text box.)

5. Click the **OK** button. Invitees appear in the All Attendees list in the Plan a Meeting dialog box. The icons to the left of their names indicate whether a meeting invitation by e-mail will be sent to them as well as their status (organizer, required attendee, optional attendee, or resource). When you point to any of these icons, a ScreenTip appears to identify that icon.

   Trouble? If the Microsoft Office Internet Free/Busy dialog box opens, click the Cancel button.

6. Set the Meeting start time for **next Tuesday** at **10 a.m.** and the Meeting end time for **next Tuesday** at **1 p.m.** The proposed meeting time, as indicated by the time between the green and red indicator lines, overlaps the time of the tentative meeting (indicated by the time block colored with blue and white stripes) you scheduled for next Tuesday.

7. Change the Meeting start time to **next Wednesday** at **10 a.m.** The new date and time does not overlap with any other meetings in your Calendar.

8. Click the **Make Meeting** button. A new Meeting window opens with the invited attendees' names and e-mail address automatically inserted in the To text box.

   As with an appointment, you must specify the meeting subject, location, and so forth.

9. Type **Web Site Expansion** in the Subject text box.

10. Type **Lucinda's Office** in the Location text box.

Next you'll insert the notes you jotted down earlier into the meeting invitation. You can insert any item into another as text, as an attachment, or as a shortcut. For example, if you wanted to include an agenda, meeting minutes, or other information that invitees should review before the meeting, you could attach a file to your meeting request, just as you would attach a file to any other e-mail message.

To insert notes text into a meeting invitation:

1. Click **Insert** on the menu bar, and then click **Item**. The Insert Item dialog box opens.

2. Click the **Text only** option button in the Insert as section of the dialog box, click **Notes** in the Look in list box, press and hold the **Ctrl** key as you click both yellow notes to select them, and then release the **Ctrl** key. See Figure 2-21.

Insert Item dialog box 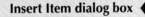 Figure 2-21

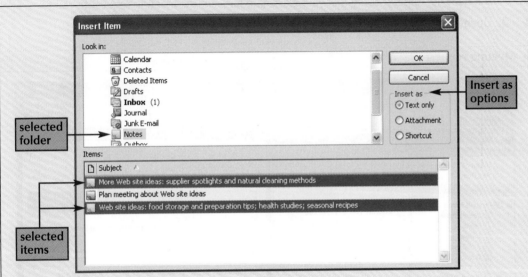

3. Click the **OK** button. The notes' appear in the text box at the bottom of the Meeting window.

You finish scheduling the meeting by sending the meeting request to the Outbox and closing the dialog box.

To finish scheduling the meeting:

1. Click the **Send** button to move the meeting request to the Outbox.

2. Send and receive the meeting request to your server, if necessary, and then switch back to the Calendar folder.

3. Click the **Close** button in the Plan a Meeting dialog box. Next Wednesday's date is now in bold in the Date Navigator.

4. Click next Wednesday's date in the Date Navigator. The scheduled meeting appears in your calendar in the 10 a.m. to 1 p.m. time block.

You can quickly schedule a meeting with someone in your contacts list. In the Contacts folder, right-click the contact, and then click New Meeting Request to Contact on the shortcut menu.

Responding to a Meeting Request

When you receive a meeting request in your e-mail, you have three options for responding. You can accept the request, you can tentatively accept the request, you can decline the request, or you can propose a new time for the meeting. However you respond, the message is returned to the meeting organizer. The meeting organizer receives the messages in his or her Inbox, and Outlook compiles the responses in the Meeting window. The organizer can open the Meeting window and click the Tracking tab to see who has responded along with the response.

To respond to a meeting request:

1. Switch to the **Inbox**, and download your messages, if necessary.

   Trouble? If the message does not yet appear, wait a few minutes and then try again. If it still does not appear, verify that your classmate has sent the meeting request to you.

2. Open the meeting request message. See Figure 2-22.

Figure 2-22   **Meeting request**

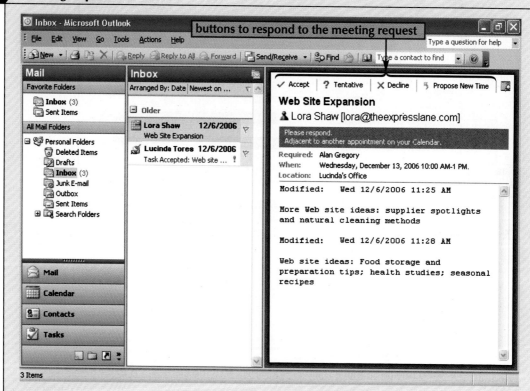

3. Click the **Propose New Time** button at the top of the message in the Reading Pane. A dialog box opens asking whether you want to use the Microsoft Free/Busy Service.

4. Click the **Cancel** button. The Propose New Time dialog box opens so you can set a new start and/or end time for the meeting.

5. Click the **Meeting start time** list arrow, and then click **10:30 AM**. The end time changes to keep the original meeting length unchanged.

6. Click the **Propose Time** button. The New Time Proposed Meeting Response window opens, so you can add a note to the message before it is sent to the meeting organizer.

7. Type **I have a conflict with another appointment. Let's start at 10:30.** in the message body. See Figure 2-23.

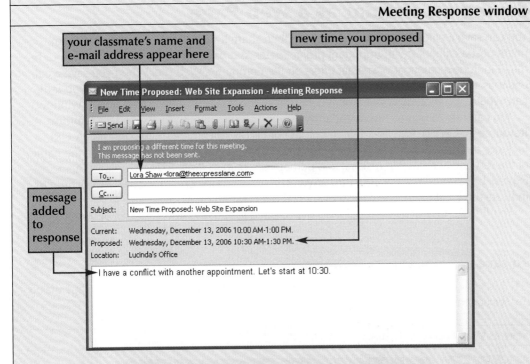

Meeting Response window | **Figure 2-23**

8. Send the message to your Outbox, send it to your server, and then download your messages, if necessary. The New Time Proposed message from your classmate appears in your Inbox.

9. Switch to the Calendar folder, click next Wednesday's date in the Date Navigator, double-click the meeting scheduled for 10:00, and then click the **Tracking** tab in the Meeting window. You see a list of the names of the meeting organizer and all attendees, the type of attendee (required, optional, or resource), and their current response (accepted, declined, tentative, or none).

10. Close the Meeting window.

Adding and Removing Meeting Attendees

After you create a meeting, you can add or remove meeting attendees and resources. To do so, open the meeting by double-clicking it in the Calendar, click Actions on the Meeting window menu bar, and then click Add or Remove Attendees. To add attendees or resources, select them and then click the Required, Optional, or Resources button as appropriate. To remove an attendee or resource, click the name in the Required, Optional, or Resources box, and then press the Delete key. Click the OK button to update your meeting.

Checking Off Completed Tasks

Because you have finished a task on your task list, you can mark it as completed. You can do this in the Tasks folder or in the TaskPad in the Calendar folder. You will mark the Plan meeting about Web site ideas as completed.

To check off a completed task:

1. In the TaskPad, click the check box next to the Plan meeting about Web site ideas task. A check mark appears in the check box, and the task is crossed out.

Saving a Calendar as a Web Page

You can save a calendar as a Web page and then share it with others. For example, Alan might post a calendar with important project dates as a page on the company intranet, or he might include a calendar of special offers on the company's Web site. When you save a calendar as a Web page, you specify the start and end dates that should display, and you indicate whether to include appointment details from the text box in the Appointment window.

You can refer others to the calendar by sending an e-mail with the calendar's **Uniform Resource Locator (URL)**, an address for a file or HTML document on the Internet. A URL includes the protocol that a Web browser uses to access the file (such as "http://"), the name of the server where the file resides, and perhaps the path to the file. For example, The Express Lane could use the URL *http://www.theexpresslane.com/calendar/specials.html* to indicate the location of its calendar of special offers found on its Web site.

You'll save next week's calendar as a Web page to see how this process works.

To save a calendar as a Web page:

▶ 1. Click **File** on the menu bar, and then click **Save as Web Page**. The Save as Web Page dialog box opens. See Figure 2-24.

Figure 2-24	Save as Web Page dialog box

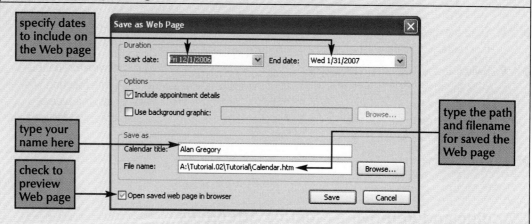

▶ 2. In the Start date list box, type **next Monday**.

▶ 3. In the End date list box, type **next Friday**.

▶ 4. Make sure that the **Include appointment details** check box is checked. This option saves the details contained in the Notes field on your calendar item, such as specifics about appointment or meeting times.

▶ 5. Type your name in the Calendar title text box, if necessary. This information becomes the name of the calendar Web page. If you do not enter a title, the user name for your computer becomes the title.

▶ 6. Click the **Browse** button, switch to the **Tutorial** folder within the **Tutorial.02** folder on your Data Disk, type **Calendar** in the File name text box, and then click the **Select** button.

▶ 7. Make sure that the **Open saved web page in browser** check box contains a check mark. After Outlook saves the calendar as a Web page, the Web page calendar will open in your browser so that you can preview it.

▶ 8. Click the **Save** button. After a moment, the saved Web page calendar opens in your browser.

▶ 9. Maximize the browser window, if necessary. See Figure 2-25.

Web page calendar in browser ◄ Figure 2-25

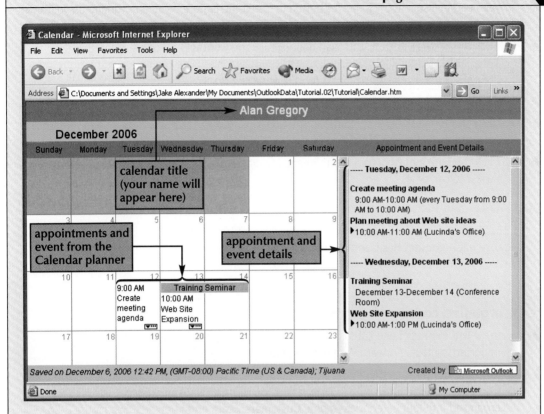

10. Preview the calendar, and then close the browser window.

The Express Lane plans to create a calendar for its Web site that includes specials, food tips, and recipes. Lucinda asks you to contact the company's suppliers and find out whether they would be willing to share food tips or recipes. Because not all suppliers have e-mail addresses, you decide to send a printed letter.

Creating a Word Mail Merge from Outlook

One way to integrate Office and Outlook is to create a form letter using the Word mail merge feature and an Outlook contact list. You can import a contact list that was created in Word, Access, or Excel into Outlook. Alan asks you to import an Access database containing the contact information for some of The Express Lane's staff, customers, and suppliers.

To import a contact list from Access:

► **1.** Create a subfolder named **The Express Lane** that contains **Contact Items** placed within the **Contacts** folder to store the imported contact items.

► **2.** Click **File** on the menu bar, and then click **Import and Export**. The first dialog box in the Import and Export Wizard opens.

► **3.** Click **Import from another program or file** in the Choose an action to perform list box, if necessary, and then click the **Next** button.

► **4.** Click **Microsoft Access** in the Select file type to import from list box, and then click the **Next** button.

Trouble? If a dialog box opens with the message that the feature is not currently installed, you need to install it. Click the Yes button to install the feature if you are working on your own machine; if you are working in a lab, ask your instructor or technical support person for help.

5. Click the **Browse** button, and then double-click the **Contacts** database located in the **Tutorial.02\Tutorial** folder included with your Data Files. The File to import text box shows the path, such as *A:\Tutorial.02\Tutorial\Contacts.mdb*.

6. Click the **Next** button.

7. Click **The Express Lane** subfolder in the Contacts folder in the Select destination folder list box, and then click the **Next** button.

8. Click the **Finish** button. In a few moments, Outlook converts the information from the database into contacts.

The list of contacts that Alan asked you to import includes more than just suppliers. Because each contact has been assigned a category, you can organize all of the contacts by category. You do this by changing the view.

To organize contacts by category:

1. Click **The Express Lane** subfolder in the My Contacts pane in the Navigation Pane. The imported contacts appear in the main window.

2. Click the **Contacts** button in the Navigation Pane, if necessary, and then click the **By Category** option button in the Current View pane in the Navigation Pane. The contacts are organized into four categories—none, Customers, Staff, and Suppliers. See Figure 2-26.

Figure 2-26	Imported contacts

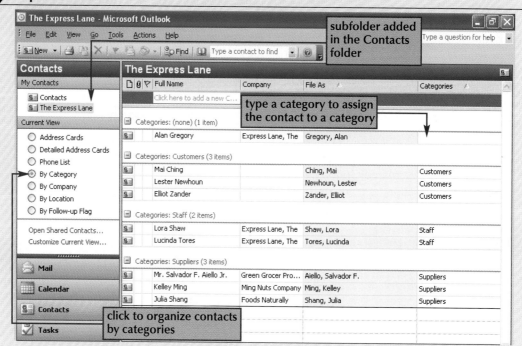

Trouble? If the categories are collapsed and the contacts are not visible, click the plus sign buttons next to the category heads to expand each category.

The contact for Alan Gregory does not have an assigned category. You assign categories to contacts just as you do other items.

4. Click in the **Categories** text box for the Alan Gregory contact, type **Staff**, and then press the **Enter** key. The category is added to the contact and the contact is moved to the appropriate category group.

Filtering and Sorting Contacts

Because you want to send the letter only to the suppliers, you'll filter the view. A **filter** displays only those items in a folder that match certain criteria. For example, you'll filter the contacts to display only the ones assigned to the Suppliers category. The other contacts remain in the folder but are not visible until you remove the filter. A filter applies only to the current view.

Reference Window

Filtering and Sorting a View

- Click the Customize Current View link in the Current View pane in the Navigation Pane.
- Click the Filter button, set filter criteria on tabs, and then click the OK button.
- Click the Sort button, set one or more sort by items, and then click the OK button.
- Click the OK button.

You'll set a filter for the Suppliers category.

To apply a filter:

1. Click the **Customize Current View** link in the Current View pane in the Navigation Pane. The Customize View: By Category dialog box opens.

2. Click the **Filter** button. The Filter dialog box opens, offering various ways to filter the contacts, such as by keyword, e-mail address, or date and time.

3. Click the **More Choices** tab, which provides additional filter options. See Figure 2-27.

Filter dialog box ◀ **Figure 2-27**

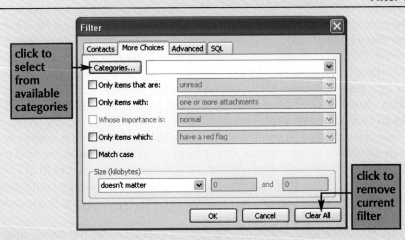

click to
select
from
available
categories

click to
remove
current
filter

4. Type **Suppliers** in the Categories text box, and then click the **OK** button to return to the Customize View: By Category dialog box. You decide to sort the contacts in ascending order by company name.

▶ **5.** Click the **Sort** button. The Sort dialog box opens.

▶ **6.** Click the **Sort items by** list arrow, click **Company**, and then click the **Ascending** option button, if necessary. See Figure 2-28.

Figure 2-28 ▶ **Sort dialog box**

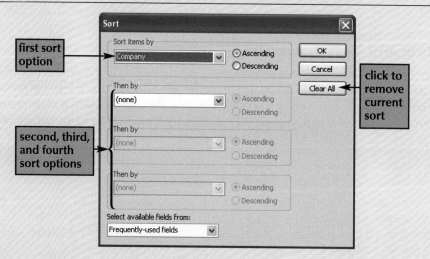

▶ **7.** Click the **OK** button. The filter and sort settings are displayed in the Customize View: By Category dialog box.

▶ **8.** Click the **OK** button. Only the contacts assigned to the Suppliers category appear in the folder, in alphabetical order by company name.

Notice that the words "Filter Applied" appear in the folder banner and the status bar to help you remember that not all the contacts are visible. These words remain until you remove the filter from the view. You're ready to create the letter with Word.

Creating the Form Letter

Outlook offers two options for writing letters. You can write a letter to one contact by selecting the contact, clicking Actions on the menu bar, and then clicking New Letter to Contact. The Word Letter Wizard opens with all of the recipient's contact information already entered. Or, you can write a personalized form letter to a group of contacts by using the Word mail merge feature. **Mail merge** is the process of combining a main document with a data source. A **main document** contains the standard text, such as the body of a letter. A **data source** is a list of variable information, such as recipient names and addresses in an Outlook contact list. To specify what information to include in the main document from the data source, you insert **merge fields**, special codes that identify the variable information that should appear in that location. When you start the mail merge process from Outlook, you determine whether to include every contact field available in Outlook or only those visible in the current view. You also choose which contacts to include in the merge—all contacts in the current view, selected contacts in the current view, or a filtered contact list.

For The Express Lane's letter, you'll use the filtered contact list as the data source so that you include only the three suppliers.

To create a mail merge form letter:

1. Click **Tools** on the menu bar, and then click **Mail Merge**. The Mail Merge Contacts dialog box opens. See Figure 2-29.

Mail Merge Contacts dialog box | **Figure 2-29**

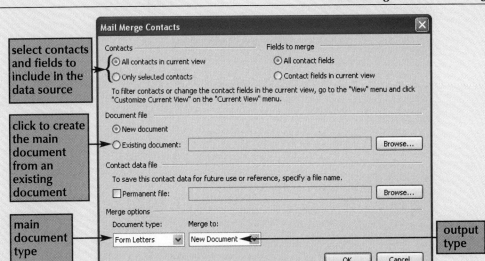

select contacts and fields to include in the data source

click to create the main document from an existing document

main document type

output type

2. Click the **All contacts in current view** option button, if necessary, and then click the **All contact fields** option button, if necessary.

3. Click the **Existing document** option button, click the **Browse** button, and then double-click the **Letter** document located in the **Tutorial.02\Tutorial** folder included with your Data Files. You'll edit the letter that Lucinda started rather than writing a new letter.

   Next you select the type of main document you want to create and the final output. The main document types—form letters, mailing labels, envelopes, and catalog—and the output options—new document, printer, and e-mail—are the same as those available in Word.

4. If necessary, select **Form Letters** in the Document type list box, and **New Document** in the Merge to list box.

5. Click the **OK** button. The letter opens in Word with the Mail Merge toolbar open.

Now you can finish the form letter by inserting the proper fields for the inside address and salutation of a business letter.

To insert merge fields in Word:

1. Click the second blank line below the date, and then click the **Insert Address Block** button on the Mail Merge toolbar. The Insert Address Block dialog box opens so you can select the format and contents of the inside address. See Figure 2-30.

| Figure 2-30 | Insert Address Block dialog box |

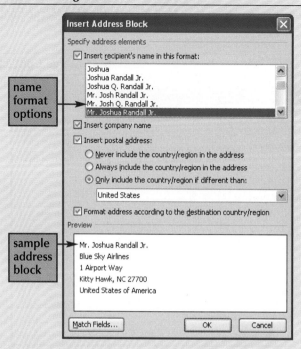

2. Verify that the dialog box selections match those shown in Figure 2-30, and then click the **OK** button. Next you insert the name field for the salutation.

3. Click after the word "Dear", press the **spacebar**, and then click the **Insert Greeting Line** button 📄 on the Mail Merge toolbar. The Greeting Line dialog box opens so you can select the format for the salutation. See Figure 2-31.

| Figure 2-31 | Greeting Line dialog box |

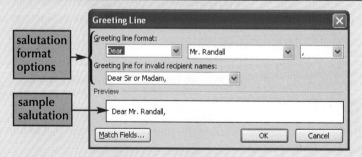

The salution "Dear" is already in the letter, so you don't need to include that as a part of your greeting line.

4. Click the first list arrow, and then click **(none)**.

5. Click the **OK** button. Figure 2-32 shows the letter with the inserted merge fields.

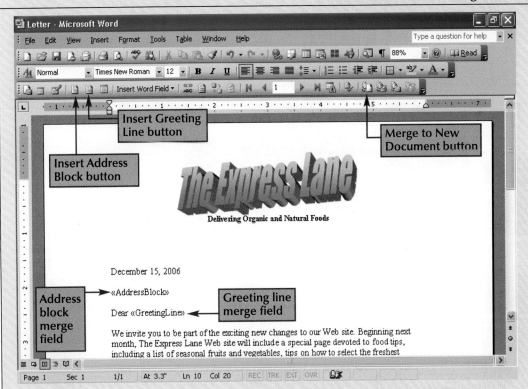

5. Press the **Ctrl+End** keys to move to the end of the letter, and then type your name.

6. Click the **Merge to New Document** button 🔲 on the Mail Merge toolbar. The Merge to New Document dialog box opens, so you can verify the settings.

7. Click the **All** option button, if necessary, and then click the **OK** button. The completed form letters appear in a new document.

8. Scroll down to see all the form letters addressed to the three suppliers, click the **Save** button 🔲 on the Word Standard toolbar, and then save the merged document as **Web Site Letters** in the **Tutorial.02\Tutorial** folder included with your Data Files.

9. Click the **Close** button ☒ on the title bar for the Web Site Letters document to close the document, click the **Close** button ☒ on the title bar for the Letter document, click the **No** button to close the document without saving, and then exit Word.

Recording the Letter in the Journal

The Journal is a diary that records the dates and times of all your interactions, items, documents, and activities. For example, you might want to keep a record of all letters you just sent to The Express Lane's suppliers. You can have the Journal record activities automatically, such as e-mail messages, meeting requests and responses, task requests and responses, and documents created in Access, Excel, PowerPoint, and Word. Also, you can manually record an activity in the Journal.

Because you want to connect the Journal entry to a contact, you'll start the entry from the Contacts folder. Otherwise, you can use the New button to start a blank entry.

To record an activity in the Journal:

1. Right-click the **Salvador Aiello** contact, and then click **New Journal Entry for Contact** on the shortcut menu. A Journal Entry window opens, with the subject and company information entered from the contact card, the current date and time, and Mr. Salvador F. Aiello Jr. listed in the Contacts text box at the bottom of the window. You need only to enter the specifics about the letter you sent. See Figure 2-33.

Figure 2-33 Journal Entry window

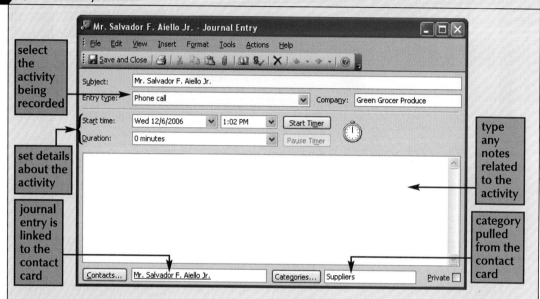

3. Click the **Entry type** list arrow, and then click **Letter**.

4. Click in the notes text box, and then type **Letter invited participation in tips and hints page on the Web site.**

5. Click the **Save and Close** button on the Standard toolbar to close the window.

6. Double-click the **Salvador Aiello** contact card to open the Contact window, and then click the **Activities** tab. The Journal entry you just created appears in the list. See Figure 2-34.

Figure 2-34 Activities tab in the Contact window

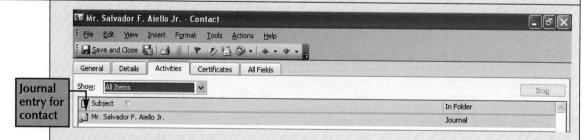

7. Click the **Save and Close** button on the Standard toolbar to close the Contact window.

Another way to track tasks, appointments, e-mail, notes, or documents related to a contact is to **link**, or connect, them to the contact. When you create an Outlook item, such as a task, you can link it to the related contact by entering the contact's name in the Contacts text box. You can also link any existing item to a contact. First, open the contact to which you want to link an item. Click Actions on the Contact window menu bar, point to Link, and then click Items. Change the Look in box to display the folder that contains the items you want to link, and then select one or more items in the Items list. You can then open the contact from any linked item just by clicking the contact's name in the Contacts box.

Removing a Filter and Sort

You've created the letters for the contacts in the Suppliers category, so you can remove the filter to display all the contacts and reset the default sort for the view. You clear both the filter and the sort in the Customize View dialog box.

To remove a filter and a sort:

1. Click the **Customize Current View** link in the Current View pane in the Navigation Pane. The Customize View dialog box opens.
2. Click the **Filter** button to open the Filter dialog box, click the **Clear All** button, and then click the **OK** button.
3. Click the **Sort** button to open the Sort dialog box, click the **Clear All** button, and then click the **OK** button.
4. Click the **OK** button in the Customize View dialog box. Outlook returns the view to its default sort and filter settings.

Communicating with Instant Messages

You can use Outlook to send and receive instant messages over the Internet. **Instant messaging (IM)**, also called chatting, is an interactive communication tool you use to converse in real time with someone over the Internet. From Outlook, you can use Microsoft Windows Messenger, Microsoft MSN Messenger (or Microsoft Exchange Instant Messaging Service) to exchange instant messages with one to four people at a time. Any message you type appears almost instantly on the computer of the other person or persons you specify. Similarly, what they type appears on your computer. If your computer has a microphone and speakers, you can speak rather than type your messages. If you have a video camera set up on your computer, the other person can see you as you exchange messages. An indicator shows when someone is responding to your message.

Once you are logged onto Windows Messenger, you can see whether someone is online and their status (such as Free or Busy). You can change your status at any time based on your current availability. The service changes your status to "Away" when you've been inactive for several minutes or appear to be offline. You can select who can and cannot send you instant messages. You can also see who has added you to their contact list.

You can add the IM address of each person with whom you want to exchange instant messages on the General tab in open Contact window for that contact. Whenever you open that person's contact card or receive an e-mail from that person, an icon with his or her online status appears next to the person's name. You can send an instant message by clicking the icon.

Lucinda wants the project team to be able to communicate using instant messaging.

Using Windows Messenger

Instant messaging requires Windows Messenger. If you don't have the program installed on your computer, you must download the program from the MSN Messenger Web page. You need a .NET Passport account to use instant messaging.

Once you have Windows Messenger installed on your computer, you can start the program. A Windows Messenger icon appears at the right end of the taskbar when the software is installed and running. When you want to use Windows Messenger, you need to sign in by supplying the e-mail address and password you entered when you registered for a .NET Passport. You can then create your list of authorized users or contacts.

Reference Window	**Using Windows Messenger for Instant Messaging**

- Double-click the Windows Messenger icon at the right end of the taskbar (*or* click the Start button on the taskbar, point to All Programs, and then click Windows Messenger).
- Click the Click here to sign in link, type your Passport e-mail address in the E-mail address text box, type your Passport password in the Password text box, and then click the OK button.
- Click the Add a contact link in the Windows Messenger window, complete the Add a Contact Wizard to enter the contacts with whom you want to chat, and then click the Finish button.

You'll start by signing in to Windows Messenger, and adding your classmate as a contact with whom you want to exchange instant messages.

To sign in to Windows Messenger:

▶ 1. Double-click the **Windows Messenger** icon 🔯 at the right end of the taskbar. The Windows Messenger window opens.

Trouble? If you do not see the Windows Messenger icon, then the program is probably not running. Click the Start button on the taskbar, point to All Programs, click Windows Messenger, and then continue with Step 2. If you don't have the program installed on your computer and you have access to install software on your computer, start Internet Explorer, go to *www.microsoft.com*, link to the Windows Messenger page, and then download and install the latest Windows Messenger program. If you do not have access to install software, you can read but not complete the rest of the steps in this section.

▶ 2. Click the **Click here to sign in** link. The Sign in to .NET Messenger Service – MSN Messenger dialog box opens.

Trouble? If you do not see the Click here to sign in link, you are already connected. Skip Steps 3 and 4, and then compare your screen to Figure 2-35.

Trouble? If the Sign in to .NET Messenger Service - MSN Messenger dialog box does not open and the Windows Messenger dialog box changes to indicate that your are online, skip Steps 3 and 4, and then compare your screen to Figure 2-35.

Trouble? If the .NET Passport Wizard opens, you do not have a .NET Passport added to your Windows XP user account. Click the Add a .NET Passport to your Windows XP user account option button, click the Next button, and then follow the wizard steps, making sure the Associate my Passport with my Windows user account check box is checked. Skip Steps 3 and 4, and then compare your screen to Figure 2-35.

You need to enter the e-mail address and password that you used when you registered for your Passport.

▶ 3. Type your Passport e-mail address in the E-mail address text box, and then type your Passport password in the Password text box.

▶ 4. Click the **OK** button. The IM features appear in the Windows Messenger window. See Figure 2-35.

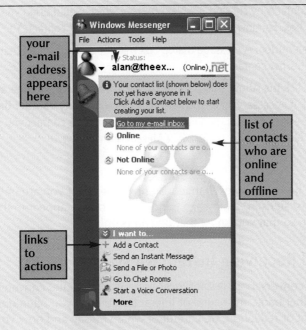

Adding an Instant Message Contact

The Windows Messenger window shows your current status and lists your contacts who are currently online and offline. It also provides links for adding contacts to your list, sending an instant message, sending a file or photo, creating or entering a chat room, starting a voice conversation, adding a group, sending e-mail, and starting a NetMeeting. For some of these activities, you'll need access to other files, programs, and equipment.

You'll add a classmate as a contact with whom you want to exchange instant messages.

To complete the steps in this section and the steps in the Sending and Receiving Instant Messages section, you'll need to work with a classmate. If you don't have a classmate to work with, ask you instructor for an e-mail address and create a contact card using that name and e-mail address. Otherwise, you should read but not complete the steps in this section and in the Sending and Receiving Instant Messages section.

To add a contact to Windows Messenger:

1. Click the **Add a Contact** link in the Windows Messenger window. The Add a Contact Wizard opens.

2. Verify that the **By e-mail address or sign-in name** option button is selected, and then click the **Next** button.

3. Type your classmate's e-mail address in the text box, and then click the **Next** button.

   Trouble? If a dialog box opens telling you that your classmate has added you to his or her contact list, click Allow this person to see when you are online and contact you option button, if necessary, click the Add this person to my contact list check box to remove the check mark, and then click the OK button. Then click the Next button in the dialog box in which you typed your classmate's e-mail address.

   The next dialog box tells you that your classmate was successfully added to your list. If you want, Windows Messenger will send an e-mail message to that e-mail address if that person is not already using Windows Messenger. You don't need this message sent.

▶ 4. Click the **Next** button. A dialog box opens telling you that You're Done! You could continue to add more contacts by clicking the Next button, which would bring you back to the first wizard dialog box. For now, you do not want to add another contact. You're finished for now.

▶ 5. Click the **Finish** button. A message dialog box might open indicating that your classmate has added you to his/her contact list.

▶ 6. If necessary, click the **Allow this person to see when you are online and contact you** option button, if necessary, click the **Add this person to my contact list** check box to remove the check mark, and then click the **OK** button. The contact you added appears in the Online or Not Online list in the MSN Messenger window.

Contacts must be online to exchange instant messages. If you are online and someone on your contact list signs in, a message window will briefly appear in the lower right corner of your screen so that you know that person is online.

Sending and Receiving Instant Messages

Like a telephone conversation, instant messaging is immediate, convenient, and often less formal. On the other hand, the speed of interaction means you often don't have the time for deeper thought or reflection. Be careful of what you say and how you say it. With a phone call, you have the benefit using your voice to convey emotions by varying your inflection, tone, pitch and volume. When you're typing instant messages, the lack of emotion can cause a misunderstanding. To make up for this lack, users rely on a growing list of abbreviations to convey their emotions and intent. They also use abbreviations as shortcuts to longer, often used expressions, which reduces the amount of typing and speeds up the exchange. Figure 2-36 lists some common abbreviations used in instant messaging.

Figure 2-36 ▶ **Common instant messaging abbreviations**

Abbreviation	Meaning	Abbreviation	Meaning
afk	away from the keyboard	ttyl	talk to you later
brb	be right back	ty or t/y	thank you
btdt	been there, done that	wb or w/b	welcome back
btw	by the way	yw or y/w	your welcome
cy	see ya	<bg>	big grin
imho	in my humble opinion	<bs>	big smile
k	okay	<g>	grin
lol	laughing out loud	<s>	smile
rofl	rolling on the floor laughing	<vbg>	very big grin
ttfn	ta ta for now	<vbs>	very big smile

Instant messaging is fast becoming a work tool similar to the telephone. Just as it is courteous to ask someone whether you have called at a convenient time, your first message might inquire whether the person has the time and the inclination to chat at that moment. Conversely, if you receive a message at an inopportune moment, you can ignore the message or tell the other person know that you don't have time to chat at the moment. You might also want to change your status.

When you first sign in, Windows Messenger lists your status as Online. Your status will change to Away if you appear to be offline or haven't used the service in while. You can also change your status, choosing from a variety of descriptions, including Busy, Be Right Back,

On the Phone, Out To Lunch, and Appear Offline. You should change your status to reflect your current availability. This way, people know whether you are available to exchange messages or occupied in another task. Similarly, respect the status of your contacts. Do not send a message to someone whose status is Busy or On the Phone, for example.

You'll exchange instant messages with your classmate.

To send an instant message:

1. Click the **Send an Instant Message** link in the Windows Messenger window. The Send an Instant Message dialog box opens.

2. Click your classmate's e-mail address on the My Contacts tab, and then click the **OK** button. The Conversation window opens. See Figure 2-37.

Conversation window 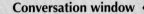 Figure 2-37

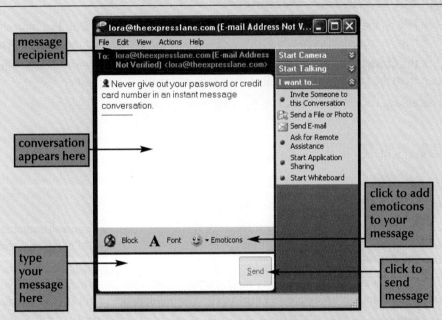

3. Type **Is this a convenient time for you to chat with me?**, and then click the **Send** button.

   Both your classmate's and your messages should appear almost instantly. Now you reply to your classmate's message.

4. Type **Yes. What's up?**, and then click the **Send** button.

   Again, the two messages appear in the Messenger window. When you no longer want to exchange messages with someone, you close the Conversation window.

5. Click the **Close** button ☒ on the Conversation window title bar.

If you want to remove a person from your contact list, you can delete the person's contact from the list.

To remove a contact from the contact list:

▶ 1. Right-click your classmate's e-mail address in the Windows Messenger window, and then click **Delete Contact** on the shortcut menu. A message balloon opens in the taskbar or a dialog box opens asking you to confirm the deletion.

▶ 2. Click the **Yes** button.

The contact is removed from the list.

When you're done exchanging messages and want to close Windows Messenger, you need to sign out. When you close Windows Messenger, the program continues to run in the Windows taskbar so you can receive instant messages once you sign in again.

To sign out of Windows Messenger:

▶ 1. Click **File** on the Windows Messenger menu bar, and then click **Sign Out**. In a moment, the Click here to sign in link appears, indicating that you have completed the sign out process.

▶ 2. Click the **Close** button ⊠ on the Windows Messenger window title bar. A message might open from the taskbar, indicating that the program will run in the taskbar.

▶ 3. If necessary, click the **Close** button ⊠ in the message balloon.

Now you will archive the Outlook items you created.

To archive the items you created:

▶ 1. Click **File** on the menu bar, click **Archive**, click the Archive this folder and all subfolders option button, click the **plus sign** button ⊞ next to Contacts in the list of folders, and then click **The Express Lane**.

▶ 2. Click the **Browse** button, navigate to the **Tutorial.02\Tutorial** folder included with your Data Files, change the filename to **Express Lane Archive**, and then click the **OK** button.

▶ 3. Type **tomorrow** in the Archive items older than text box, click the **OK** button, and then click the **Yes** button to confirm that you want to archive the folder.

▶ 4. Click the **Folder List** button ▣ in the Navigation Pane, and then click the **plus sign** button ⊞ next to Archive Folders in the Navigation Pane. The Archive Folders list expands.

▶ 5. If you don't see The Express Lane contacts folder in the expanded Archive Folders list, drag **The Express Lane** contacts folder on top of the Archive Folders in the Navigation Pane. The Express Lane contacts folder now appears as a subfolder in Archive Folders.

Now you will copy additional items into the Archive Folders.

▶ 6. Press and hold the **Ctrl** key, drag the **Tasks** folder on top of Archive Folders, and then release the mouse button and the **Ctrl** key. The Tasks folder is copied to Archive Folders.

▶ 7. Copy the **Notes** folder, the **Journal** folder, and the **Calendar** folder to Archive Folders.

▶ 8. Right-click **Archive Folders** in the Navigation Pane, and then click **Close Archive Folders** on the shortcut menu.

Before finishing, you'll remove the extra time zone and labels from the planner, and return the workday to its default setting of Monday through Friday, 8 a.m. to 5 p.m. Then you'll delete any items you've created and stored in Outlook, including the custom category you added.

To remove the Calendar customizations and delete items:

▶ 1. Click **Tools** on the menu bar, click **Options**, and then if necessary click the **Preferences** tab.

▶ 2. Click the **Calendar Options** button. The Calendar Options dialog box opens.

▶ 3. Click the **Sat** check box to remove the check mark.

▶ 4. Change the **Start time** to **8:00 AM** and the **End time** to **5:00 PM**.

▶ 5. Click the **Time Zone** button. The Time Zone dialog box opens.

▶ 6. Delete **Here** from the top Label text box, delete **Athens** from the additional time zone Label text box, and then click the **Show an additional time zone** check box to remove the check mark.

▶ 7. Click the **OK** button in the Time Zone dialog box, click the **OK** button in the Calendar Options dialog box, and then click the **OK** button in the Options dialog box.

▶ 8. Click **View** on the menu bar, and then click **TaskPad** to close the TaskPad. The Calendar is returned to its default settings.

▶ 9. Right-click any item, click **Categories** on the shortcut menu, click the **Master Category List** button, click the **Reset** button, click the **OK** button to confirm the return to the default list, and then click the **OK** button in each dialog box.

▶ 10. Delete the contact card that contains your own information, the four tasks from the Tasks folder, and the three notes from the Notes folder by clicking each item and then clicking the **Delete** button ⊠ on the Standard toolbar.

▶ 11. Right-click the **Create meeting agenda** appointment on next Tuesday's date in the Calendar, click **Delete** on the shortcut menu, click the **Delete the series** option button in the Confirm Delete dialog box that appears, and then click the **OK** button.

▶ 12. Right-click the other appointment on the next Tuesday's date, and then click **Delete** on the shortcut menu.

▶ 13. Right-click the **Web Site Expansion** meeting on Wednesday's date, click **Delete** on the shortcut menu, click the **Delete without sending a cancellation** option button in the warning dialog box that opens, and then click the **OK** button.

▶ 14. Right-click the **Training Seminar** event on next Wednesday's date, and then click **Delete** on the shortcut menu.

▶ 15. Click the **Journal** folder in the Navigation Pane, click the **No** button in the warning dialog box that opens asking if you want to turn the Journal on, right-click the **Entry Type: Letter** item, click **Delete** on the shortcut menu, and then click the **OK** button in the warning dialog box that opens.

▶ 16. Empty the Deleted Items folder.

The redesign of The Express Lane's Web site is off to a good start. Lucinda, Alan, and Lora are looking forward to the next month's meetings to finalize the page content and design.

Session 2.2 Quick Check

Review

1. What is the purpose of the AutoPick feature?
2. True or False? Once you invite people to a meeting, you cannot remove them from the meeting attendee list.
3. Describe the steps for saving a calendar as a Web page.

4. What does a mail merge do?
5. True or False? You cannot remove a filter after you have applied it to a view.
6. Explain how an instant message is different from an e-mail message.

Review

Tutorial Summary

In this tutorial, you created notes and organized them with categories. You created a task list and assigned a task to someone else. You scheduled appointments and events in the Calendar. You planned a meeting and saved your calendar as a Web page. You merged a Word letter and Outlook contact list to create form letters. You created a Journal entry to record an activity for a contact. Finally, you used Windows Messenger to chat with a classmate in real time.

Key Terms

appointment	filter	recurring task
AutoCreate	instant messaging (IM)	task
AutoDate	link	task request
AutoPick	mail merge	TaskPad
category	main document	Uniform Resource
data source	meeting	Locator (URL)
event	merge field	
Field Chooser	recurring appointment	

Practice

Practice the skills you learned in the tutorial.

Review Assignments

Data File needed for the Review Assignments: Contacts.xls

Lucinda Tores asks you to work with her to plan how to inform customers about the new features on The Express Lane's Web site. You'll create a schedule for the coming days and then prepare mailing labels for the letters Lucinda plans to send to customers.

1. Create a contact card for yourself, using your name and e-mail address.
2. Create a blue note with the text "Write letter to customers to inform them of our new Web site features," add yourself as the contact, and then close the note.
3. Create a green note with the text "Get customer comments and recipes for the Web site," add yourself as the contact, and then close the note.
4. Create a task from the blue note with a due date of tomorrow that is assigned to the Customer category. (*Hint:* You will need to create an entry in the Master Category List.)
5. Create a task with the subject "Import updated contact list" and a due date of today. Assign the task to the Customer category.
6. View the tasks By Category.
7. Customize your calendar so that the workweek includes Monday through Saturday and workdays start at 7 a.m. and end at 8 p.m.
8. Schedule an appointment for the Import updated contact list task for tomorrow morning between 10 and 10:15, do not enter a location, and turn off the reminder. (*Hint:* Type the end time in the right End time text box in the Appointment window to create a 15-minute appointment.)
9. Create a two-day event with the subject "Storing, cooking, and eating artichokes" that begins three days from now. Turn off the reminder for this event.

10. Create a recurring appointment to attend the event both days between 10 a.m. and 1 p.m.
11. Print your calendar for one day on which you have scheduled appointments and events.

For Steps 12 through 14, you need to work with a classmate.

12. Schedule a one-hour meeting for tomorrow at 1 p.m. with a classmate, with the subject "Discuss customer suggestions for Web site."
13. Insert the green note as an attachment in the notes text box of the meeting request, and then send the meeting request. (Click the Yes button in the dialog box that warns that the recipient might not be able to receive the attachment.)
14. Decline the meeting request you receive.
15. Save your calendar for this week and next week as a Web page, using the filename **Schedule** and saving it in the **Tutorial.02\Review** folder included with your Data Files, and preview the page in your Web browser. Close the Web page and the browser.
16. Create a subfolder named "Lucinda" that contains Contact Items placed within the Contacts folder, and then import the contact list from Microsoft Excel called **Contacts** located in the **Tutorial.02\Review** folder included with your Data Files.
17. Display the TaskPad, and then check off the "Import updated contact list" task as completed.
18. Filter the contact list in the Lucinda subfolder to display only contacts in the Customer category.
19. Start a mail merge using all contacts in the current view and all contact fields, create a new document for the mail merge using Mailing Labels as the document type, merge to a New Document, and then click the OK button.
20. Click the OK button in the message dialog box to open the Mail Merge Helper dialog box. Click the Setup button in the Mail Merge Helper dialog box. Click 5160 - Address in the Product number list, and then click the OK button. Click the Edit button in the Main document section, and then click Mailing Label: Document1. Insert the Address Block merge field in the first label, click the Propagate Labels button on the Mail Merge toolbar, and then merge the labels to a new document.
21. Save the merged document as **Customer Address Labels** in the **Tutorial.02\Review** folder included with your Data Files, and then close it. Close the main document without saving it, and then exit Word.
22. Create a journal entry for the activity of creating address labels in the Elliot Zander contact.
23. Remove the filter from the contact list in the Lucinda subfolder.

For Steps 24 through 25, you need to work with a classmate.

24. Sign in to Windows Messenger, add a classmate to the contacts list, and then exchange instant messages with your classmate about how to inform customers about the new features on The Express Lane's Web site, using appropriate abbreviations.
25. Remove your classmate from your contacts list, sign out of Windows Messenger, and then close Windows Messenger.
26. Archive the Lucinda contacts folder and save the archive in a file named **Review Archive** in the **Tutorial.02\Review** folder included with your Data Files. Copy the Notes, Tasks, Journal, and Calendar folders into the new Archive Folders that you created.
27. Reset the calendar workweek to Monday through Friday, the start time to 8 a.m. and the end time to 5 p.m., delete all the items you created in these assignments, including the category you added to the master list, the Lucinda subfolder, and the contact card you created with your own information, and then empty the Deleted Items folder and close the Archive Folders.

Case Problem 1

Data File needed for this Case Problem: Answers.mdb

Answers Anytime Answers Anytime, an online tutorial service, staffs its offices 24 hours a day, 7 days a week. Renna Necone organizes the staff schedule using the Calendar, saves it as a Web page, and then posts the schedule on the company intranet. This week, Answers Anytime is hosting an all-day seminar about Greek and Roman mythology.

1. Create a yellow note with the text "Prepare chart comparing the Greek and Roman names of gods."
2. Create a task from the note with a due date of next Wednesday and a High priority.
3. Assign the task to a classmate. Accept the task request that you receive.

Explore

4. Create a second task with the subject "Set up next week's schedule" and a due date of four hours from now. (*Hint:* Type "four hours from now" in the Due date text.) Assign the task to a new category you create called "Schedule."
5. Create a subfolder named "Answers Anytime" that contains Contact Items placed within the Contacts folder, and then import the Access database contact list **Answers** from the **Tutorial.02\Cases** folder included with your Data Files into the subfolder.
6. Set up a schedule for the staff for next Monday through Friday. Each shift lasts eight hours and recurs every two days. Show the time as Free. (*Hint:* Look in the Answers Anytime subfolder to review the staff list.)

Explore

7. Link each series of recurring appointments to a staff member in the Answer Anytime subfolder. Double-click each recurring appointment, click the Open the series option button in the Open Recurring Item dialog box, and then click the OK button. Next, click the Contacts button at the bottom of the Appointment window, display and click the Answers Anytime folder in the Look in list, and then click a staff member's name in the Items list box.
8. Create an event for next Friday called "Mythology Seminar," and turn off the reminder.
9. Plan a staff meeting for next Tuesday from 10 a.m. to 11 a.m. with the entire staff of Answers Anytime as Required Attendees in the Conference Room.

Explore

10. In the Plan a Meeting dialog box, change the e-mail icon in the first column for each required attendee to Don't send meeting to this attendee. (*Hint:* Click the e-mail icon, and then click the appropriate option in the list.)

Explore

11. Send the meeting requests. Because you selected the Don't send meeting to this attendee option, no recipient names are entered in the To text box in the meeting request e-mail, and a dialog box or message balloon opens. Click the Yes button to confirm that you want to save and close the meeting instead.
12. Print next week's calendar in the Weekly Style.
13. Save next week's calendar as a Web page with the filename **AnswersSchedule** in the **Tutorial.02\Cases** folder included with your Data Files, and preview the page in your browser. Close the browser window.

Explore

14. Write a letter to Benji Tanago that asks him to create a table comparing the Greek and Roman names of gods. From the Answers Anytime contact subfolder, click Benji's contact card, click Actions on the menu bar, click New Letter to Contact, and then follow the instructions in the Letter Wizard in Word. Save the letter as **Greek and Roman Gods** in the **Tutorial.02\Cases** folder included with your Data Files.
15. Print the letter, and then exit Word.
16. View the activities for three contacts in the Answers Anytime subfolder.
17. Archive the Answers Anytime contacts folder using the filename **Answers Anytime Archive** in the **Tutorial.02\Cases** folder, and then add a copy of the Notes, Tasks, and Calendar folders to the archive.

18. Delete the items that you created in this Case Problem, close the Archive Folders, and then empty the Deleted Items folder.

Case Problem 2

Create

Create notes, tasks, and a schedule for graduation party.

Data File needed for this Case Problem: Guest List.mdb

Party Planners   Jace Moran uses Outlook to plan a graduation party, including its time and date. Jace asks you to jot down ideas for the party's theme, create a task list, and then schedule time to complete those tasks. The party will take place next Friday evening.

1. Create at least two notes containing ideas for the party. For example, one note might suggest possible party themes or include a reminder to send directions to party guests.
2. Create a task list of at least four activities that Jace must complete before the party. For example, she might need to finalize the number of guests and provide that information to a caterer.
3. Schedule an appointment for the party and then schedule appointments to complete each task during the week before the party, setting appropriate time and label colors.
4. Create a subfolder named Party Guests in the Contacts folder that contains Contact Items, and then import the contact list from Microsoft Access called **Guest List** located in the **Tutorial.02/Cases** folder included with your Data Files.
5. Assign the category "Key Customer" to one contact who is the client for whom you are planning the party.
6. Create a category called "Guests," and then assign it to the other contacts.
7. Filter the contact list to display only contacts assigned to the Key Customer category.
8. Plan a final appointment with the client. (*Hint:* Use the customer in the Key Customer category.)
9. Insert any appropriate notes into the notes text box of the Appointment window.
10. Print the calendar for the week of the party, using the Daily Style.
11. Remove the filter from the Party Guests contacts subfolder.

For Steps 12 through 15, you need to work with a classmate.

12. Sign in to Windows Messenger, and then add a classmate to the contacts list.

Explore ▶ 13. Exchange instant messages with your classmate about the graduation party's theme and tasks that need to be completed. Use appropriate abbreviations and emoticons. (*Hint:* Click the Emoticon button in the Conversation window, and then click an emoticon button to insert that icon into your message at the location of the insertion point.)

Explore ▶ 14. Go to the Windows Messenger window, change your status to On The Phone, and then have your classmate send you an instant message to see what happens. (*Hint:* Click File on the menu bar, point to My Status, and then click On The Phone.)

Explore ▶ 15. Save your conversation as a text file with the filename **Party Conversation** in the **Tutorial.02\Cases** folder included with your Data Files. (*Hint:* Click File on the Conversation window menu bar, and then click Save.)

16. Remove your classmate from your contact list, sign out of Windows Messenger, and then close the Windows Messenger window.
17. Archive the Party Guests folder as **Party Guests Archive** in the **Tutorial.02\Cases** folder, and then copy the Notes, Tasks, and Calendar folders to the Archive Folders.
18. Delete all the items that you created in this Case Problem, close the Archive Folders, and then empty the Deleted Items folder.

Quick Check Answers

Session 2.1

1. True
2. A task is a one-time item on your to-do list that you want to perform. A recurring task occurs repeatedly.
3. The AutoCreate feature converts the note to a new task.
4. A category is a way to assign items a keyword or phrase that you can then use to organize and locate related items.
5. An appointment is an activity that does not involve other people or resources. An event is an activity that lasts one or more full days. A meeting is an appointment with other people or resources.
6. blue-striped

Session 2.2

1. The AutoPick feature finds the best time for a meeting by locating the first available free time for all people and resources invited to the meeting.
2. False
3. In the Calendar folder, click File, Save as Web Page, choose a start and end date, choose whether to include appointment details, type a Calendar title, choose the location to which you want to save the Web page, choose whether to open the new Web page in a browser window, and then click the Save button.
4. Mail merge combines a main document of standard text (such as a letter written in Word) with a data source of variable information (such as an Outlook contact list).
5. False
6. An instant message appears on the recipient's screen almost as soon as you press Send; an e-mail message resides on the recipient's server until the recipient downloads his or her e-mail messages.

Glossary/Index

Note: Boldface key terms include definitions.

A

account name. *See* user ID

address. *See* e-mail address

appointment An activity that you schedule in your calendar but that does not involve other people or resources. OUT 60

    recurring, OUT 68–69

    scheduling, OUT 65–69

archive A feature that lets you manually transfer messages or other items stored in a folder (such as an attachment in the e-mail folder) to a personal folder file when the items have reached the age you specify. OUT 41–42

Archive dialog box, OUT 41–42

arrangement A predefined arrangement of how items in a view are displayed. OUT 38

ascending order Arranges messages alphabetically from A to Z, chronologically from earliest to latest or numerically from lowest to highest. OUT 38

assigning tasks, OUT 57–58

attachment A file that you send with an e-mail message. OUT 27–28

AutoCreate An Outlook feature that generates a new item when you drag an item from one folder to another. OUT 55

AutoDate An Outlook feature that converts natural-language date and time descriptions, such as one week from today and noon, into the numerical format that represents the month, day, and year or time, respectively. OUT 57

AutoPick A feature that selects the next available free time for all invitees and resources. OUT 71

C

Calendar An Outlook folder in which you use a calendar to schedule appointments, events, and meetings. OUT 4, OUT 60–70

    configuring options, OUT 61–65

    navigating within, OUT 60–61

    printing calendars, OUT 70

    scheduling appointments, OUT 65–69

    scheduling events, OUT 69

Calendar Options dialog box, OUT 62

calendars, saving as Web pages, OUT 76–77

Categories dialog box, OUT 53

category A keyword or phrase that you assign to an item to help organize and later locate related items, regardless of whether they are stored in the same folder. OUT 52

    organizing contacts, OUT 78–79

    organizing notes, OUT 52–53

    organizing tasks, OUT 58–59

Check Full name dialog box, OUT 16

coloring e-mail messages, OUT 39–40

contact Each person or organization with whom you communicate. OUT 14–20

    creating, OUT 15–19

    distribution lists, OUT 20–23

    editing, OUT 19–20

    fields, OUT 14

    filtering and sorting, OUT 79–80

    IM, OUT 87–88

    organizing by category, OUT 14–20 OUT 78–79

    sending contact information by e-mail, OUT 20

contact card All of the information about a contact. OUT 18

Contacts An Outlook folder in which you store information about the people and businesses with whom you communicate, similar to an address book. OUT 4

Create New Folder dialog box, OUT 31

D

data source A list of variable information, such as recipient names and addresses in an Outlook contact list. OUT 80

deleting

    items in Outlook, OUT 42

    rules, OUT 42

    signatures, OUT 43

descending order Arranges messages in reverse alphabetical, chronological, or numerical order. OUT 38

Detailed Address Cards view, OUT 18–19

displaying. *See* viewing

distribution list A group of people to whom you frequently send the same messages. OUT 20–23

E

editing contacts, OUT 19–20

Edit Signature dialog box, OUT 9–10

e-mail The electronic transfer of messages between computers.

    attachments, OUT 27–28

    coloring messages, OUT 39–40

    creating messages, OUT 10–12

    filing messages, OUT 31–34

    finding messages, OUT 34–37

    flagging messages, OUT 29–30

    forwarding messages, OUT 25, OUT 26

    importance setting, OUT 12

    message body, OUT 11

    message format, OUT 8–9

    messages archiving, OUT 41–42

    organizing/managing messages, OUT 30–34

    printing messages, OUT 26

    receiving, OUT 23–25

    replying to messages, OUT 25

    sending messages, OUT 13–14

    sensitivity level, OUT 12, OUT 13

    setting up accounts, OUT 7–8

    signatures, OUT 9–10

    sorting messages, OUT 38–39

    stationary, OUT 10

    storing messages, OUT 40–42

e-mail address A user ID and a host name separated by the @ symbol. OUT 7

emoticon Punctuation marks and other characters arranged to look like a face turned sideways; used to convey emotion; also called smiley. OUT 11

event A one-time or annual activity that lasts 24 hours or more, such as a seminar, trade show, or vacation. OUT 60

    scheduling, OUT 69

exiting Outlook, OUT 43

Task Reference

TASK	PAGE #	RECOMMENDED METHOD
Archive folder, close	OUT 41	Right-click Archive Folder in Folder List, click Close "Archive Folder"
Arrangement, switch	OUT 38	Click View, point to Arrange By, click desired arrangement
Attachment, add to e-mail	OUT 27	From Message window, click 📎, select file location, double-click file to insert
Attachment, save	OUT 28	Right-click attachment icon in Reading Pane or Message window, click Save As, select save location, enter filename, click Save
Attachment, view	OUT 28	Double-click attachment icon in Reading Pane or Message window, click Open, click OK
Contact, create	OUT 15	See Reference Window: Creating a Contact
Contact, edit	OUT 20	Switch to Address Cards or Detailed Address Cards view, click in contact card, edit text as usual, click outside contact card
Contact, forward as vCard	OUT 20	Click contact card in Contacts folder, click Actions, click Forward as vCard
Contact, forward by e-mail	OUT 20	Right-click contact card in Contacts folder, click Forward
Contacts view, change	OUT 18	Click Contacts button in Navigation Pane, click option button in Current View pane
Deleted Items folder, empty	OUT 43	Right-click Deleted Items folder in All Folders pane in Navigation Pane, click Empty "Deleted Items" Folder, click Yes
Distribution list, create	OUT 21	See Reference Window: Creating a Distribution List
Distribution list, modify	OUT 23	Double-click distribution list contact in Contacts folder, click Select Members to add more contacts, click Remove to delete selected contact
E-mail, receive	OUT 23	Switch to Mail folder, click Send/Receive button on Standard toolbar
E-mail account, set up new account	OUT 7	Click Tools, click E-mail Accounts, follow wizard to Add a new e-mail account
E-mail message, create	OUT 11	See Reference Window: Creating an E-mail Message
E-mail message, format	OUT 12	Select text, click appropriate buttons on Formatting toolbar in Message window
E-mail message, forward	OUT 26	Select message, click Forward button on Standard toolbar in Inbox, enter recipient e-mail address(es), type message, click Send button on toolbar in Message window
E-mail message, open	OUT 28	Double-click message in Inbox main window
E-mail message, print	OUT 26	Select message in Inbox main window, click File, click Print, verify printer,
E-mail message, read	OUT 24	Click message in Inbox main window, read message in Reading Pane
E-mail message, reply	OUT 25	Select message, click Reply button on Standard toolbar in Inbox, type reply message, click Send button on toolbar in Message window
E-mail message, send to Outbox	OUT 13	Click Send button on toolbar in Message window

TASK	PAGE #	RECOMMENDED METHOD
E-mail message, set importance	OUT 12	Click ⚠ or ⬇ on Standard toolbar in Message window
E-mail message, set sensitivity	OUT 13	Click Options button on toolbar in Message window, select sensitivity level in Sensitivity list in Options dialog box, click OK
E-mail messages, send from Outbox	OUT 13	Switch to Mail folder, click Send/Receive button on Standard toolbar
Flag, add reminder to message in Inbox	OUT 29	Right-click flag icon in message header in Inbox main window, click Add Reminder, select or type a message in Flag to list, select due date in left Due by list, select due time in right Due by list, click OK
Flag, add to message in Inbox	OUT 29	Right-click flag icon in message header in Inbox main window, click desired flag color
Flag, mark complete	OUT 30	Click flag icon in message header in Inbox until check mark appears
Folder, create	OUT 31	Right-click folder in Navigation Pane, click New Folder, type folder name, select items you want to store in Folder contains list, select folder location, click OK
Folder List, display	OUT 6	Click 📁 in Navigation Pane
Folder List, use	OUT 6	Click folder in Folder List pane; click ➕ to see nested folders
Forwarded contact card, add to Contacts folder	OUT 20	Drag contact card attachment from Message window to Contacts folder
Items, delete	OUT 43	Click item, click ✖, click Yes if necessary
Items, select multiple	OUT 43	Click first item, press and hold Ctrl key, click additional items, release Ctrl key
Message format, choose	OUT 8	Click Tools, click Options, click Mail Format tab, select HTML in the Compose in this message format list, click OK
Messages, archive manually	OUT 41	Click File, click Archive, click Archive this folder and all subfolders option button, click folder to archive, type date in Archive items older than text box, click Browse, select save in location, click OK, click OK, click Yes
Messages, color	OUT 39	Click Tools, click Organize, click Using Colors link, set options, click Apply Color
Messages, file	OUT 31	Select message or messages in main window, drag to appropriate folder or subfolder
Messages, find	OUT 34	See Reference Window: Finding Messages
Messages, save	OUT 40	See Reference Window: Saving Messages in Another File Format
Messages, sort	OUT 38	Click column heading
Messages, sort by two or more columns	OUT 38	Click column heading, hold down Shift, click additional column headings, release Shift
Navigation Pane, use	OUT 6	Click button in Navigation Pane, click folder if necessary
Rule, create simple	OUT 33	See Reference Window: Creating a Simple Rule

Task Reference

TASK	PAGE #	RECOMMENDED METHOD
Rule, delete	OUT 42	Click Tools, click Rules and Alerts, click rule in Rule list box, click Delete, click Yes, click OK
Search Folder, display new	OUT 36	Right-click Search Folders in All Mail Folders pane in Navigation Pane, click New Search Folder, click desired Search Folder, click OK
Search Folder, use preset	OUT 36	Click ⊞ next to Search Folders in All Mail Folders pane in Navigation Pane, click Search Folder
Signature, create new	OUT 9	Click Tools, click Options, click Mail Format tab, click Signatures, click New, enter a name for signature, click desired starting point option, click Next, type signature text, add font and paragraph formatting as needed, click Finish, click OK, click OK
Signature, delete	OUT 43	Click Tools, click Options, click Mail Format tab, click Signatures, click signature in Signature list box, click Remove, click Yes, click OK, click OK
Signature, select for e-mail account	OUT 10	Click Tools, click Options, click Mail Format tab, select e-mail account name in Select signatures for account list, select signature in Signature for new messages list, select signature in Signature for replies and forwards list, click Apply, repeat for other accounts, click OK
Stationery, create an e-mail message with	OUT 10	In Inbox, click Actions, point to New Mail Message Using, click More Stationery, select desired stationery, click OK
vCard, forward by e-mail	OUT 20	Click contact card in Contacts folder, click Actions, click Forward as vCard
View, switch	OUT 38	Click View, point to Arrange By, point to Current View, click desired view
Word, choose as e-mail editor	OUT 8	Click Tools, click Options, click Mail Format tab, check the Use Microsoft Office Word 2003 to edit e-mail messages check box, click OK